# Integration in Practice

The report of a national study to identify common areas of quality in early years and childcare

*Early Childhood Unit, National Children's Bureau*
*on behalf of the Department for Education and Employment*

**NATIONAL**
**CHILDREN'S**
**BUREAU**

Early Childhood Unit

NCB promotes the interests and well-being of all children and young people across every aspect of their lives. We advocate the participation of children and young people in all matters affecting them. We challenge disadvantage in childhood.

NCB achieves its mission by
- ensuring the views of children and young people are listened to and taken into account at all times
- playing an active role in policy development and advocacy
- undertaking high quality research and work from an evidence based perspective
- promoting multidisciplinary, cross-agency partnerships
- identifying, developing and promoting good practice
- disseminating information to professionals, policy makers, parents and children and young people

NCB has adopted and works within the UN Convention on the Rights of the Child.

Published by National Children's Bureau Enterprise, the trading company for the National Children's Bureau, Registered Charity number 258825
ISBN 1 900990 21 0
© National Children's Bureau, 2000
8 Wakley Street, London EC1V 7QE
Printed by Page Bros, Norwich
Front cover photograph: Courtesy of NES Arnold
Photograph on page 89 by Adrian Rowland (National Children's Bureau, 1998)

Early Childhood Unit, National Children's Bureau

# Contents

# List of tables and figures

## Tables

## Figures

# About the authors

**Ann Jamieson** is the Director of the Early Childhood Unit at the National Children's Bureau

**Claire Cordeaux** is the Joint Commissioning Manager, Suffolk Social Services and Suffolk Health Authority

**Lucy Wilkinson** is a Project Development Officer in the Early Childhood Unit at the National Children's Bureau

# Acknowledgements

None of this work would have been possible without the enthusiastic collaboration of our colleagues in the Local Authority Early Years Coordinators' Network and the Early Years Development and Childcare Partnerships. We appreciate that the materials that contributed to the report may have subsequently been updated since the time of going to print.

We are also grateful to the Department of Education and Employment for their continued support of the Integration in Practice project. Thanks are also due to Sue Stern from the DfEE and to Elspeth Davies from OFSTED for their cooperation throughout the project. We would like to thank the staff of the Early Childhood Unit, in particular Ann Robinson, Sue Owen, Gemma Stunden and Patricia Thomas, and also Diane Rich for her time. Final thanks are due to NES Arnold for their allowing us to reproduce the beautiful Puppet Girl.

# Introduction

This report is the culmination of a year-long study, funded by the Department of Education and Employment (DfEE), that looked at the state of play of integration in early years education and care and found local diversity running hand in hand with a deep national consensus on what is good for children. With the imminent transfer of responsibility for Part X of the Children Act 1989 from local authorities to OFSTED, the findings of the study have the potential to provide a new basis for the further development of integrated, holistic services.

Essentially Integration in Practice sought to:
- identify materials used as a basis for integrated practice to support the learning of children from birth to 14-years-old;
- audit these materials and identify common elements and examples of good practice;
- conduct regional seminars to discuss findings and reach consensus on elements of good practice;
- aggregate and disseminate the findings in a national report;
- establish a web-accessed evidence site for the interactive and ongoing development of good practice.

The materials collected included: curriculum guidance; daycare standards; quality assurance materials; Early Years Development and Childcare Partnership plans, audits and other documents, in particular kitemark schemes where they existed; underpinning principles for Partnership work; materials being developed. There was almost equal representation of care (Registration and Inspection) and education materials and almost a quarter of these came from Early Years Development and Childcare Partnerships (EYD&CPs). Education materials mostly focussed on children aged three to five, Registration and Inspection materials on children from birth to eight-years-old, and Partnership materials on children from birth to 14-years-old.

All local authorities, including the LEAs and Registration and Inspection units, and their respective Partnerships in England, were contacted. The regional response rate was extremely good with an average rate of 68 per cent of all local authorities returning their documents. Attendance at the 18 regional seminars, or focus groups, and the final national discussion group was equally good with more than 70 authorities being represented at the final discussion.

An audit instrument was designed, deriving from existing government guidance such as: the National Curriculum; the Desirable Learning Outcomes and subsequently the Early Learning Goals; The Children Act 1989; the National Occupational Standards. It also derived from theoretical approaches such as: High/Scope; Effective Early Learning (Pascal, 1994); Aiming for Quality (Pre-School Learning Alliance, 1996); Quality in Diversity (Early Childhood Education Forum, 1998). Some international approaches were also utilised, such as Te Whakiri from New Zealand; Reggio Children from Italy; Social Educators/ Forest Kindergarten from Denmark.

Using a reflexive process of analysis, by auditing and discussing successive sets of findings, the researchers progressively focussed all of the quality materials into 69 Common Quality Areas. A full explanation of these is available in Chapter 2. In each instance, the Common Quality Area is described as a summary of the *range* of meanings covered within the materials audited. These ranges of meaning are sometimes contradictory but, nevertheless, they represent the common body of thinking which is guiding current practice in the majority of early education and childcare provision in England.

The identification of this degree of commonality offers a powerful platform for further development of practice in the UK. For instance, from a further clustering of the Common Quality Areas, the researchers were able to propose a group of eight overarching areas described as Organising Principles (see Chapter 3). The idea was that such a group of principles, transparently rooted in the diversity and traditions of local practice, could act as a bridge between standardised national systems of quality control (for registration and external inspection to be carried out by OFSTED) and local systems of quality assurance (emanating from the EYD&CPs, Local Authorities and individual settings, including childminders).

The development of these possibilities begins in Chapter 1, which reviews the thinking underpinning approaches to quality and seeks to provide a broad framework for the subsequent analysis of the approaches evident in the contributions of the local authorities and Partnerships included in the study. Existing DfEE guidance is also considered in this context with the aim of signposting links between the required work of the Partnerships and the broader literature of quality.

Chapter 2 sets out the project methodology and comments on the appropriateness of qualitative methods for the analysis of practitioner views and written materials intended to guide practice. The resultant findings are included in Chapter 3, where you will find all of the 69 Common Quality Areas listed with an analysis of their respective range of meaning. Chapter 3 also includes a review of the 18 regional focus group discussions and the final national focus group, which were held to refine emergent findings throughout the project.

Chapters 4 and 5 detail examples of local quality assurance frameworks and written guidance within the 69 Common Quality Areas, quoting directly from materials analysed within the project. Finally, a series of next steps are proposed in Chapter 6, which sets out a possible new national framework for the achievement of quality and suggests how the electronically stored evidence of the Integration in Practice project can be used to further develop good practice.

# 1. Approaches to quality

The year 2000 is likely to see the Care Standards Bill passing onto the Statute Book and the subsequent transfer of responsibility for Part X of the Children Act 1989 to OFSTED under the control of Her Majesty's Chief Inspector of Schools. This shift represents the culmination of what could be described as the final phase of the present government's manifesto commitments to improving early years and childcare services. As such, it is likely to put in place the final pieces of infrastructure that will support these services and their future development for some years to come. It is timely, therefore, that this study offers a position statement on progress towards the integration of education and care that has been the spur for these changes.

The Integration in Practice Project has been predicated on the understanding that the achievement and experience of quality can be best found in the interactions between adults and children and that quality is a complex and multidimensional concept which comprises values, cultural expectations, aspirations and diverse professional discourses, as well as more formal systems of regulation and enforcement. This chapter will explore the components available, or soon to become available, for the construction of a national system for the continuous achievement of quality. It will briefly consider the current literature on ways of thinking about quality and address how the findings of this study might offer a platform for future development.

## National policy on integrated provision

*Early Excellence: A head start for every child* (Labour Party, 1996) published by the Shadow Labour Cabinet anticipated the creation of a new system of integrated provision, characterised by settings providing both care and education (exemplified by a string of Early Excellence Centres) and a unified process of registering and inspecting them. Much has happened since the Early Excellence initiative, some of which goes beyond its central vision. Many national agendas can now be seen to converge on early years and childcare, not least of which is the drive to eradicate child poverty and Welfare to Work. Since May 1997, one initiative has followed close on the heels of another so that at this moment in time any consideration of quality must acknowledge the National Childcare Strategy, the Working Families Tax Credit, Best Value, the National Literacy and Numeracy Strategies, developments in health services, Quality Protects and so on. Against this background, the drive for *quality* begins to be possibly the single most powerful force available to us in bringing the experience of children into meaningful focus. Quality therefore must become a broad strategy stretching far beyond the boundaries of early years and childcare settings and engaging all the stakeholders including parents and children.

Whereas the national regulator (OFSTED) will be independent of most of the support and development infrastructure, it is nevertheless generally recognised that there is a need for an identified framework to facilitate the relationship between policy initiatives, the varying organisational structures across England (voluntary, independent and maintained) and regulation, registration and inspection. There must be a continuous system in order for quality

to be achieved. Without such a national regulatory system, it is unlikely that the whole will be greater than the sum of the parts.

## Guidance relating to children's learning

The greater part of this study has been the audit and analysis of the written documentation that underpins each particular set of local expectations or ambitions authority by authority, Partnership by Partnership, region by region, and on a national level from constituent professional discourses. As we shall see later in this report, there is a wide consensus within this literature, and the conversations surrounding it, upon what is good for children. As a first step in undertaking the analysis, an audit classification was devised based on the following sets of approaches to children's learning (see Tables 1.1 and 1.2). The findings set out in Chapter 3 describe all the resultant 69 Common Quality Areas distilled from the local, though nonetheless 'top down', aspirations for quality in our sample.

**Table 1.1    National guidance relating to children's learning**

| DLOs (SCAA, 1996) | Early Learning Goals (QCA, 1999a) | National Curriculum (Statutes, 1998) | National Occupational Standards (Statutes, 1998) | Children Act 1989 (Statutes, 1989) |
|---|---|---|---|---|
| Personal and social development<br><br>Language and literacy<br><br>Mathematics<br><br>Knowledge and understanding of the world<br><br>Physical development<br><br>Creative development | Aims are to:<br>• foster personal, social and emotional well-being<br>• promote positive attitudes to learning in all children<br>• enhance social skills in all children<br>• promote attention skills and persistence in all children<br><br>*A teaching programme…*<br>• Language and communication, reading and writing<br>• Mathematics<br>• Knowledge and understanding of the world<br>• Physical development<br>• Creative development | Religious education<br><br>*Core subjects*:<br>English<br>Mathematics<br>Science<br><br>*Foundation subjects*:<br>Technology/Art<br>Music<br>History<br>Geography<br>Physical Education | *Principles:*<br>• The welfare of the child<br>• Keeping children safe<br>• Working in partnership with parents/families<br>• Children's learning/development<br>• Equality of opportunity<br>• Anti-discrimination<br>• Celebrating diversity<br>• Confidentiality<br>• Working with other professionals<br>• The reflective practitioner | • Standards in daycare Services for Under 8s and educational provision for the Under 5s<br>• Children's welfare and development are paramount<br>• Children should be treated/ respected as individuals whose needs (inc. SEN) should be catered for<br>• Parents' responsibility recognised and respected<br>• Values from different backgrounds recognised and respected<br>• Parents as first educators of children<br>• Parents' access to information<br><br>*Standards:*<br>• Staffing: ratios and fit persons<br>• Premises/space<br>• Maximum places<br>• Size of group<br>• Furniture/equipment<br>• Toys<br>• Snacks and meals<br>• Observation and records<br>• Relationship with parents<br>• Visits and outings |

DLO = Desirable Learning Outcomes
QCA = Qualifications and Curriculum Authority
SCAA = School Curriculum and Assessment Authority

**Table 1.2    Independent approaches to children's learning**

| High/Scope (Brown, 1990) | Montessori Education (1995) | Effective Early Learning Project (Pascal, 1994) | Quality in Diversity (ECEF, 1998) | Pre-School Learning Alliance (1996) |
|---|---|---|---|---|
| Room arrangement in areas<br><br>The daily routine<br><br>Plan – Do – Review<br><br>• Key experiences<br>• Creative representation<br>• Language and literacy<br>• Initiative and social relations<br>• Movement<br>• Music<br>• Classification<br>• Seriation<br>• Number<br>• Shape<br>• Time | *Children explore a broad range of subjects:*<br><br>• Own choices<br><br>• Practical Life tasks<br><br>• Language<br><br>• Mathematics<br><br>• Geography/History/ Biology/Botany/ Zoology/Art/Music | *Ten dimensions of quality:*<br>• curriculum/ learning experiences<br>• planning, assessment and record keeping<br>• aims and objectives<br>• monitoring and evaluation<br>• parental partnership, liaison and coordination<br>• equal opportunities<br>• relationships and interactions<br>• staffing<br>• teaching and learning styles<br>• physical environment | *Foundations for early learning:*<br><br>• Belonging and connection<br>• Being and becoming<br>• Contributing and participating<br>• Being active and expressing<br>• Thinking, imagining and understanding<br><br>Goals for early learning | • Creative and aesthetic development<br>• Emotional development<br>• Language and literacy<br>• Mathematics<br>• Moral and spiritual experience<br>• Moving towards independence<br>• Physical development<br>• Science<br>• Social and human development<br>• Technology |

# Political goals

We have also been interested to explore the ways in which each set of written materials links aspirations for quality with active mechanisms to achieve it. In this regard we have attempted to discover how, and by whom, each set of materials has been produced and how they have been applied in practice. Consciously or unconsciously, each set of materials relies on local process and it is likely that the more explicitly this process is articulated, the more effective the measures contained within them are likely to be.

Inherent in the literature on quality is an assumption that actions to secure or assure quality have political direction. By this we mean that quality systems exist within the overall aspirations of those who operate them in order to reach specific policy objectives that derive from political imperatives. In his influential book, *The Learning Game* (1996), Michael Barber argues that the political conflict over education in the post-war era can be described within a classification taken from *1066 and All That*. Essentially he states that those on the political right have tended to believe that the major goal of education should be diversity, even if it went hand in hand with inequality. He goes on to say that the political left has been characterised by an 'argument that the overarching goal of education should be equality even if the consequence of the pursuit of equality was uniformity'. Using the *1066 and All That* classification that the Cavaliers were 'wrong but romantic' and that the Roundheads were 'right but repulsive', he therefore gave the following diagram:

**Figure 1.1    Classification of political goals in education**

|  | INEQUALITY | EQUALITY |
|---|---|---|
| DIVERSITY | Wrong<br>but<br>romantic | Right<br>and<br>romantic |
| UNIFORMITY | Wrong<br>and<br>repulsive | Right<br>but<br>repulsive |

*(Barber, 1996)*

What this can be taken to mean in the context of frameworks for quality is that the pursuit of equality is the political and policy goal and that the preferred organising principle for this should be diversity of provision not uniformity of provision. Barber's argument is essentially that equality can be pursued across diverse types of provision. Quality systems to ensure that this happens would involve checking both that diverse provision exists and that all children have access to the same entitlement to education irrespective of the provision offered. In such a system, benchmarking across different types of institution would rely on the measurement of common outcomes for their respective children. One could argue that the present system of league tables, comparing exam performance and other tests across schools, does exactly this. Political goals cannot be separated from quality systems and the Organising Principles driving them. Quality systems will tend to act to ensure the delivery of political goals, whether this is explicitly articulated or not, and much of the literature about quality in early years and childcare, with its emphasis on the rights of children and parents, reflects this understanding.

## Frameworks for quality

Our starting point is that any discussion of quality must take account of a number of separate elements and that these are:

- regulation (including registration and inspection);
- national standards;
- guidance;
- levels of organisation including individual settings or childminders, networks or chains of settings or childminders (including those which are led by private enterprises), services or other structural arrangements within local authorities, local authorities, Early Years Development and Childcare Partnerships, regional structures, structures within national government, structures external to but linked to national government, for example, the Qualifications and Curriculum Authority and the Early Years National Training Organisation;
- national programmes and policy initiatives including the National Childcare Strategy, Sure Start, New Deal, New Deal for Communities, Supporting the Family, the National Curriculum and the Foundation Stage, Health Improvement Strategies, the modernisation of local government and Best Value;
- the distinct professional discourses including care, play, education and disability;
- the qualifications and training levels of the workforce;

- the pay and conditions of the workforce;
- the professional associations and trades unions which are aligned with the distinct professional discourses;
- the distinct bodies of literature which fall within the generic title of quality;
- training and development;
- processes and structures, and the related literature of these;
- beliefs and values;
- political interest.

Whilst these elements are not all of equal weight and influence, it is not always clear which are the dominant influences at any single point in time. Professional autonomy, for instance, may be set high on the agenda within professional associations but given less prominence within an Early Years Development and Childcare Partnership (EYD&CP). What we also know, however, is that no matter what is written about the 'should' of practice, at the end of the day it is what guides and motivates the individual nursery nurse, teacher or childminder that will determine the quality of children's experiences. What we also know is that these face-to-face workers are subject to many influences, only a few of which can be measured within existing formal mechanisms. In considering the elements available to us for the achievement of quality, it is therefore vital that elusive and ambiguous phenomena, such as culture and ethos, are also included.

There is a subjective aspect to quality that is elusive, but nevertheless powerful. It is not uncommon for many experienced practitioners, when asked to describe how they understand quality, or know when it is present, to say 'you can feel it'. Indeed, within this project we have found many instances where whole integrated frameworks, such as that in use in Leeds, describe quality as being 'like beauty in the eye of the beholder'. This essentially subjective characteristic is very much in evidence in the materials we have analysed and in the focus group discussions we have conducted.

## Education, care and play

Early years education, childcare and play services have separate aetiologies and disparate professional groupings, associations and interests. Yet the literature of quality across the constituent sectors and professions now insists that care, education and play are inseparable. There are important milestones in national policy that reflect this thinking. *Starting with Quality* (Department of Education and Science, 1990), the report of the Committee of Inquiry into the Quality of Educational Experience Offered to Three- and Four-Year-Olds argued that play-based education was the right of all children. Simultaneously, the Children Act (1989) put the provision of day care and services to support children from birth to eight and their families at the centre of what was intended to be a continuum of locally flexible services. *The Children Act Guidance* (Department of Health, 1991) for these services laid the foundation for much of what we have today and was clear that childcare should have an articulated educational component.

The big messages of the Children Act were partnership, prevention and the paramountcy of children's welfare. Common principles across divergent professional practice were intended to replace compartmentalised systems that had often put children's needs at the mercy of disparate theories, protocols and professional interests.

As Under Fives services changed to Under Eights services following the Children Act, local authority activity became more coherent and was given a higher profile (not least through the three-yearly Section 19 Review of Services for Children Under Eight). Few social services departments ever fully implemented the intentions of the Children Act in terms of the prioritisation of a preventive continuum, but in a significant number of authorities the opportunity to integrate education, care and play was not missed. There is now some semblance of a developed model of integrated services in many authorities, although it is true to say that none of them are exactly the same.

The requirement to review all services, whether in the private, voluntary or statutory sector, to publish results and make information available to parents was taken seriously in many local authorities. There can be few who doubt the influence of this on the thinking of those responsible for the provision of services. Being required to think across all sectors has provoked different strategies for expansion, far more so, of course, than if local authorities had been left only to think within their own boundaries. A similar influence is also evident in the approach to registration and inspection that has evolved within local authorities.

However, as we have said, changes in policy infrastructure or organisation are only part of the story. Professional practice in the UK is profoundly influenced by what we described as the 'professional discourse'. Here, the great milestones of the last decade (that is since Rumbold (DES, 1990)) begin with the *Start Right Report* (Ball, 1994) commissioned by the Royal Society of Arts and chaired by Sir Christopher Ball. Arguing for the integration of education and care, Start Right's fundamental principles were that:

- Early childhood is the foundation on which children build the rest of their lives. But it is not just a preparation for adolescence and adulthood: it has an importance in itself.
- Children develop at different rates, and in different ways, emotionally, intellectually, morally, socially, physically and spiritually. All are important: each is interwoven with others.
- All children have abilities that can (and should) be identified and promoted.
- Young children learn from everything that happens to them and around them; they do not separate their learning into different subjects or disciplines.
- Children learn most effectively through actions, rather than from instruction.
- Children learn best when they are actively involved and interested. Children who feel confident in themselves and their own ability have a head start to learning.
- Children need time and space to produce work of quality and depth.
- What children can do (rather than what they cannot do) is the starting point in their learning.
- Play and conversation are the main ways by which young children learn about themselves, other people and the world around them.
- Children who are encouraged to think for themselves are more likely to act independently.
- The relationships children make with other children and with adults are of central importance to their development.

*(Ball, 1994)*

With this sort of thinking already in place, it is probably not surprising that the *Desirable Outcomes for Children's Learning before Compulsory School Age* (Qualifications and Curriculum Authority, 1996) produced to govern the standards of delivery of free sessional nursery education places within the nursery voucher scheme prompted outrage from many professional interests. However, for the voluntary and private sector providers who previously felt excluded from what they saw as the 'closed shop' of education, the goals were seen as a stepping stone to recognition.

The present Labour government has actively sought to address the disparities within its own programme and, apart from the Partnerships, plans, Early Excellence Centres and the Early Learning Goals, we now have the Early Years National Training Organisation and a new move to integrate the regulatory framework. However, the national pattern of services is still characterised by the different histories of its components. Whilst very serious efforts are being made within the Early Excellence Centres and many of the local authorities to integrate education and care, the National Childcare Strategy and the provision of early education for three- and four-year-olds are separately funded and continue to be driven by separate central government targets. Meanwhile, Sure Start is the major initiative for children from birth, and although Early Years Development and Childcare Plans must cover all these developments, they continue to have lives and budgets of their own. There are also substantial developments in health and social services that are tending to separate traditional relationships between services for 'children in need'.

Perhaps more significantly, efforts to match workforce skills to the demands of integration continue to be confronted with huge pay, conditions and training issues. Although we have had integrated early years degrees for several years, we are no nearer to having a new kind of worker than when rationalisation was first mooted in the then Strathclyde Region in the 1980s (Penn, 1992). Efforts within the Strathclyde Under Fives Service to rationalise care and education posts met with massive resistance from many quarters and since then even the most adventurous services in the 'integrated' authorities have sought only to combine teaching and care in different kinds of combined centres or networks. As evidenced by current DfEE guidance, which requires qualified teacher input into all early education provision, and the Early Excellence Centres' efforts to unite teaching and care into unified systems, it is unlikely that the model of integration aspired to in England (and perhaps all the UK) will include a new pedagogue, although this is the logical conclusion to be drawn from much of what is written about the best ways of supporting children's learning and developing citizenship.

Of course it is constantly argued that the UK falls short of the levels of quality in integrated care and education already attained in its partner EU countries. As early as March 1992 a *Council of Ministers Recommendation* (Council of European Communities, 1992) had proposed specific objectives for developing services for young children:

- affordability;
- access to services in all areas, both urban and rural;
- access to services for children with special needs;
- combining safe and secure care with a pedagogical approach;
- close and responsive relations between services, parents and local communities;
- diversity, flexibility of services and increased choice for parents;
- coherence between different services.

As the following two tables show, we still have a largely uncoordinated mix of services and a significantly under-qualified workforce.

**Table 1.3**    **Under Fives and Pre-school Services, England 1998 (NCB, 2000)**

| POPULATION | ENGLAND |
|---|---|
| Total population[1] | 49,495,000 |
| Population age 3- and 4-years-old [2] | 1,326,400 |
| Population age birth to 4-years-old | 3,248,200 |
| Population age 4-years-old | 674,900 |
| Under Fives (as % of total population) | 6.56 |
| **CHILDMINDERS** [3] | |
| Registered childminders | 94,700 |
| Places (a) | 370,700 |
| Places per 100 children age from birth to 4-years-old | 11.41 |
| **DAY NURSERIES** [3] | |
| Local authority day nurseries (b) | 500 |
| Places in local authority nurseries | 18,670 |
| Places per 100 children age from birth to 4-years-old | 0.57 |
| Registered private nurseries | 6,100 |
| Places in registered private nurseries | 203,000 |
| Places per 100 children age from birth to 4-years-old | 6.25 |
| **PLAYGROUPS** [3] | |
| Playgroups | 15,700 |
| Places | 383,600 |
| Places per 100 children age 3- 4-years-old | 28.92 |
| Children using playgroups (c) | 690,480 |
| as % of 3- and 4-year-olds | 52.06 |
| **NURSERY SCHOOLS AND CLASSES** [4] | |
| Nursery schools | 533 |
| Full time pupils in nursery schools | 8,247 |
| Part time pupils in nursery schools | 40,389 |
| Total pupils in nursery schools | 48,636 |
| Nursery classes | 6,015 |
| Full time pupils in nursery classes | 30,662 |
| Part time pupils in nursery classes | 289,060 |
| Total pupils in nursery classes | 319,722 |
| Total pupils in nursery schools/classes | 368,358 |
| as % of 3- and 4-year-olds | 27.77 |
| **INFANT CLASSES** [4] | |
| Under 5s, full time | 321,122 |
| Under 5s, part time | 30,998 |
| Under 5s, total | 352,120 |
| as % of 3- and 4-years-old | 26.55 |
| as % of 4-years-old (d) | 52.17 |
| **INDEPENDENT SCHOOLS** [4] | |
| Under 5s, total | 52,252 |
| as % of 3- and 4-year-olds | 3.94 |

*Notes on Table 1.3*

**General note on fluctuations in statistics**
(This note was appended to analyses in previous years, and may still apply)

Some figures may show unusual variations from those for previous years. All the source documents cited below point out that the registration exercise under the Children Act 1989 had been taking place during this period, and that the accuracy of the registers, and therefore of the figures collected, varied greatly between local authorities. For example, some premises or providers registered under the 1948 Act may no longer have been providing services, but had not previously been excluded because there was no annual inspection. Also, some nursery schools previously registered as playgroups are now excluded. The source documents advise that changes should be treated with caution.

(a)  Since 1992 places with childminders have been recorded for children from birth to seven rather than only for those under five. Notes accompanying the figures for England state that seven percent of childminder places were registered for children under five only, three per cent for children age five to seven only, but that the great majority of places – 90 per cent – were not specific to either age group. It is reasonable to assume that the majority of these places are actually used by children under five. The percentages in this summary are therefore still given as for children under five.

(b)  Since 1992 information has been collected about the number of family centres operated by local authorities, and for 1998 (England) this shows 400 centres (3). Workplace nurseries may be included in returns for day nurseries. Working for Childcare's 1995 survey showed 561 employer-sponsored nurseries in England and Wales.

(c)  The Pre-school Learning Alliance estimates that 1.8 children use each playgroup place.

(d)  Because LEA policies regarding admission to infant/reception classes vary, it is difficult to ascertain how many children who are not yet five have been admitted at any one point in time. However, the great majority of this group of children are age four rather than three, and therefore the figures for under fives in infant classes as percentages of four year-olds more accurately reflect the situation than as percentages of three- and four-year-olds.

**References**

[1] *Population Trends,* no. 98. Winter 1999, Table 1.5 (Office for National Statistics)

[2] *Population by year bands*, Office for National Statistics, personal communication, Jan 2000

[3] *Children's Day Care Facilities at 31 Mar 1998, England* (Statistics of Education series)

[4] *Pupils under five years in each LEA, England – Jan 1997* (Statistical Bulletin 10/98). DfEE

**Table 1.4    National statistics on training**

| Occupational group | % qualified | No qualification: national variation |
|---|---|---|
| Independent day nursery | 78.8% | 29% in Northern Ireland<br>26% in Scotland<br>20.3% in England<br>19.5% in Wales |
| Pre-school/playgroups | 74.3% | England only |
| Classroom assistants | 29.5% | England only |
| Nursery nurses in schools | 87.9% | England only |
| Out-of-school clubs | 57.4% | England only |
| Childminders | 31/7% | England only |

*Hera 2 Final Report* (Cordeaux, 1999)

In 2000, a new Education Select Committee is undertaking an Early Years Inquiry. Notwithstanding Rumbold ten years earlier (DES, 1990), this Committee began with a brief that only considered quality issues for the provision of education for three- and four-year-olds. Significantly, however, the Committee has agreed to extend its brief to cover children from birth to eight after taking direction from a series of convergent influences. These included: *Quality in Diversity in Early Learning: A framework for early childhood practitioners* (ECEF,1998), the central policy document of the Early Childhood Education Forum; a joint submission from this Forum and the Local Authority Early Years Coordinators' Network that argued quality provision for three- and four-year-olds can only be made sense of within a 'from birth' continuum which is practice, rather than content, led; and finally the Committee were impressed by what they saw on a visit to the Peers Early Education Project in Oxfordshire which offers community-based support for a 'from birth' to three-year-old curriculum and is part of the Sure Start programme.

## Partnerships and the emerging national quality system

What then have we got which might be called a system for the achievement of quality which takes account of these separate influences and brings them into a coherent focus of action? What common understanding might hold such a system together? What is the role of quality control and quality assurance within it? Is there a universal approach to quality in the UK?

Existing Department of Education and Employment (DfEE) guidance to EYD&CPs requires that each partnership aims to ensure that their plan:

... enhances the care, play and educational experience of young children and the care and play experience of children up to 14, including those with special educational needs and those with disabilities up to the age of 16 and sets out guiding principles for quality:

- All early education and childcare should be focussed on meeting children's needs and promoting child safety and welfare;
- There should be seamless services for children bringing together play, care and education;
- Children in Government funded early years education should have access to an education programme which will help them achieve the new Early Learning Goals for the National Curriculum;
- The welfare of children in need should be safeguarded and promoted as set out in the local authority's Children's Services Plan (CSP);
- Parents and other family members should be involved in early education and childcare, and parents and other carers should have the opportunity to improve their skills by a variety of means; there should be support for informal carers, access to appropriate family learning opportunities and support for improving parenting skills;
- There should be clear criteria which describe the minimum standard of service that all providers should meet;
- There should be more uniform regulation across all sectors with improvement in quality through inspection, self-assessment and action planning;
- There should be a clear framework of qualifications for early years and childcare workers who will be encouraged to develop and seek formal recognition for their skills;
- A qualified teacher should be involved in all settings providing early years education within an Early Years Development and Childcare Plan;
- Each early education setting and approved childminding network should identify a designated member of staff to act as special educational needs co-ordinator (the SENCO).

*(DfEE, 1999)*

In addition, in Annex Five (Strategies for Quality of Services, Recruitment and Training) all EYD&CPs are required to set out their strategy to raise the quality and standards of services delivered in their area beyond minimum standards. In this, they are asked to identify targets to raise quality and it is clear that the capacity of staff to work with the Early Learning Goals (the revised version of the Desirable Learning Outcomes) in settings delivering early education, across all provider groups, is a central component. No doubt, once new national standards for registration and inspection are in place, these will be used to set expectations outside education. Partnerships are further required to outline plans to improve the integration of childcare and early education. Essentially, what this guidance allows for is the configuration of local strategies by each EYD&CP, within the terms of the DfEE guidance and using national standards as the key signposts.

What the existing guidance does not explicitly do is set out how all the separate sets of activities, which are the responsibility of different stakeholders including the Partnerships and those bodies external to them – the regulators, parents, setting staff and providers – combine within an agreed set of relationships to maximise each other's contribution. At local level, this set of relationships will either explicitly or implicitly constitute a quality process. Ultimately, it will be this process, or system of relationships, which will support (or not) the interactions between adults and children. The professional discourse that informs individual practice and the beliefs and values of the individuals will also, of course, be an essential aspect of this system of relationships.

The DfEE does, however, offer a lead on some elements of process. The institution of the Partnership in itself suggests a collaborative and participative approach to quality. Furthermore, the requirement that planning is informed by an appreciation of diversity and a guarantee of accessibility adds a distinctive push for equality that can only be interpreted as steering the process that is required. The DfEE also state at the beginning of their guidance that an important aim of the Partnerships is to 'generate genuine debate between all providers and others, and seek agreement about how those needs can best be met'. Thus, from the beginning, the DfEE is telling us that they wish to see participative and collaborative systems that can acknowledge disparate interests in the formulation of a working consensus.

So what can we conclude about the current state of play in England that confronts Partnerships in their efforts to create holistic and child-centred systems of provision? Essentially, it seems that Partnerships are being expected to design and implement local programmes to enhance quality, but in a context of considerable flux where the dilemmas about pay and conditions of staff remain unresolved, and where the traditions of care and education continue to support different and sometimes divergent interests. As we indicated above, the DfEE has acknowledged some of these disparities and is seeking to promote collaboration through the mechanism of the plans and the Partnerships themselves, taking information and understanding from the Early Excellence Centres as it becomes available. So we begin to see that the Partnerships operate on at least two levels: to bring the disparate providers together; and to generate an acceptance of participation and collaboration as part of a quality process. Although similar, these tasks are not the same.

Many of the other functions designated to the Partnerships are overlaid by the requirements of Best Value (part of the agenda for modernising local government). Best Value aims to set up a system of continuous improvement to embody an anticipated virtuous circle of activities as follows:

- **Challenge** (is it the service or policy that is needed?);
- **Compare** (compare actual performance with promises);
- **Consult** (be responsive to the needs of users, listen to and work with stakeholders, including both customers and staff);
- **Compete** (what matters is what works: the partnership and/or local authority should use the best supplier whether public, private or voluntary sector);
- **Collaborate** (work across organisational boundaries to deliver services that are shaped to user needs and policies that take an holistic approach to cross-cutting problems).

At local level a Best Value Performance Management Framework can look like this:

**Figure 1.2     The Best Value Performance Management Framework**

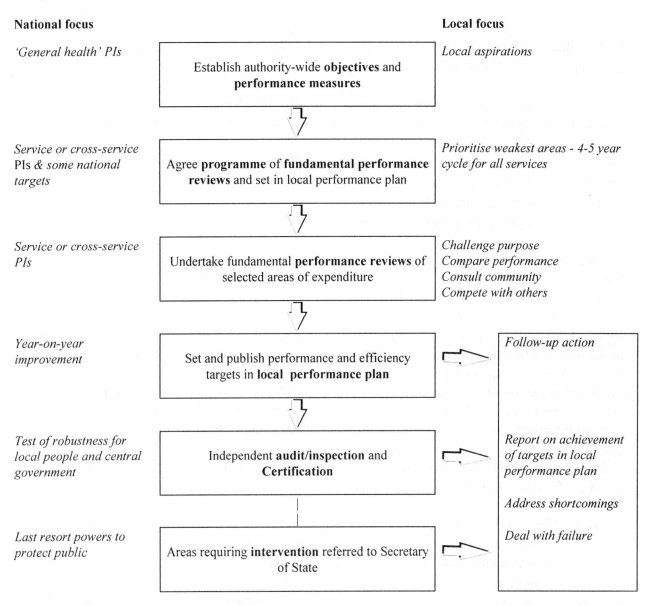

*(Department of the Environment, Transport And The Regions, 1998)*

Within this process, benchmarking is a critical function:

Bench marking can include:

- **Assessing** your organisation's present quality by comparing performance against your own objectives;
- **Diagnosing** the present level of quality by comparison with others;
- **Identifying** the 'gap' between local performance and 'best practice';
- **Establishing** what changes should, or could, be made to improve processes and reduce the 'gap';
- **Investigating** completely new ways of delivering services;
- **Setting** realistic and achievable standards;
- **Evaluating the impact** of change on key indicators and success factors.

> Bench marking is used by an outward-looking organisation which is innovative with a culture of continuous improvement and seeking to be 'the best'.

*(Puffitt, 1999)*

Partnerships and their respective local authorities, therefore, sit at the hub of several overlapping quality processes:

- one driven from within the local authority by Best Value;
- one driven by the different professional discourses of staff and their respective professional associations;
- the local wishes and expectations of parents;
- national standards, guidance and regulation;
- external registration and inspection;
- local guidance, policy and frameworks.

EYD&CPs must not only consider how these processes relate to the world of children (within Integration in Practice we have found there is a constant search for this), but also how they relate to each other so that they can be brought into a united and overarching system.

Much of the comparative methodology of Best Value will not be unfamiliar to those members of the early years and childcare community who have been engaging in 'Plan – Do – Review' (one of the shorthands for the High/Scope approach to children's learning) for years. But there is a fundamental question to be considered about the fitness for purpose of these sorts of systems and the socio-cultural needs of developing children. Beliefs and values have much to do with the quality of interactions that surround children, and children cannot determine their own in the same way as adults. Children are consulted as part of the childcare audits, but such consultation can only cover those aspects of quality that are to do with preferences, for example, for type of service.

There is a larger question about the extent to which children are able to direct their own experience, compared with adults' ability, in adult-driven systems. Quality for children needs to be addressed in ways that, for example, take account of the intimacy of their contact with adults and the long hours away from home that many of them experience. Most national policy is predicated on the principle that children's services are inherently developmental for the adults as much as for the children. Continuing professional development is therefore critical to the *evolution* of quality in services for children whereas, in many business quality systems, continuing professional development is more to do with the maintenance of existing high standards. There is also an ethical dilemma posed by systems such as Best Value if they are to be stand-alone systems for the provision of early years and childcare: all children have a right to the best possible service. To suggest in any way that it is desirable for one local authority to be seen to have superior services to the one next door is not acceptable. Early years and childcare staff must be motivated to ensure that every child has the experience of services that meet their needs. Objective measures of quality must therefore challenge the professional development of the workers in the most intimate ways. As Michael Barber has predicated, equality must be a common aspiration within the dominant political discourse of the present government.

It therefore seems as if the emergent national systems raise more questions than they answer for the Partnerships. Not only must Partnerships take stock of all the constituent influences on quality within local and national arenas, they must also think through the relationships that connect all the separate elements. More than this, as this study demonstrates, they are looking to achieve all this in ways that enable all children to have an equal chance in life. Many of the materials describing the parameters of what is regarded as good practice locally often leave these connections as assumptions and do not make explicit reference to the role of, for example, line management and organisational decision-making. Furthermore, many of the materials seek only to have influence within the classroom or playgroup and do not acknowledge external factors except perhaps for the role of staff development, but even this can be subject to a different system. What seems clear is that, if Partnerships are serious about the impact of their responsibilities for quality (and they all say they are), they must be explicit not only about what they wish to see in the experience of children but also about how this will most likely be realised. Many of the materials we have analysed in this report do not make explicit the systems and/or processes they might expect to see. However, some do have overarching systems, and in Chapter 4 we describe ten examples within a framework for analysis derived from the following approaches to quality.

## Approaches to quality

In 1991, Naomi Pfeffer and Anna Coote of the Institute for Public Policy Research published an examination of quality in *Is quality good for you?* (Pfeffer and Coote, 1991). Their central concern was to discuss the way different approaches to quality served different, and sometimes conflicting, interests. They concluded by outlining four different approaches in the existing practice:

- the **traditional approach** – which seeks to convey prestige and positional advantage;
- the **'scientific'** or **expert approach** – which seeks to conform to standards determined by experts;
- the **managerial** or **'excellence' approach** – which seeks to measure customer satisfaction, in pursuit of market advantage;
- the **consumerist approach** – which seeks to empower the customer.

*(Pfeffer and Coote, 1991)*

None of these approaches based on business goals were considered by the authors to be fit for public service purpose in ways that adequately expressed the pre-eminent drive for equality – the core value in public services or services that seek to serve the public. However, they then articulated a possible further approach:

- the democratic approach – which they argued could be used to achieve common goals in the interests of the community as a whole.

Within this last approach, Coote and Pfeiffer talk about the use of systematic auditing and the need to determine fitness for public service purpose, drawing the language of management into community-based systems. Public service purpose was to be determined by a combination of auditing and consultation that would determine a locally-defined vision for services that would then serve as the yardstick for measuring success. There are clear influences here in the Best Value approach that uses local consultation and locally-defined notions of value. There is also a resonance with the understanding that surrounds us from around the world. The often quoted

African proverb, 'It takes a whole village to raise a child', for instance, begins to sound like something which can be systematised rather than romanticised.

In 1995, Peter Williams suggested in *Making Sense of Quality: A review of approaches to quality in early childhood services* (Williams, 1995) that there are three main choices for early years and childcare services:

- **Total quality:** a relatively dynamic approach but stressing outcomes in the experience of children and staff as well as process and having the main components of: commitment, involvement, consultation, talking, working in focus groups, feedback, training and learning.
- **Quality assurance:** a more static approach with dynamic aspects; giving full weight to objective standards while trying to improve performance up to those standards and having the main components as: standards, indicators, evidence, systems, procedures, prevention, coordination, monitoring and also motivation, commitment, self-assessment and management.
- **Quality control:** a static approach, imposing objective standards independent of service providers and having as its main components: performance indicators, detailed standards, criteria for pass/fail, arms-length inspection.

*(Williams, 1995)*

Williams goes on to suggest that each of these three different kinds of approach is appropriate in different situations, that the ends justify the means.

Similar, albeit differently expressed, themes are evident in the work of Peter Moss and Alan Pence who in *Valuing Quality in Early Childhood Services* (Moss and Pence,1995), argue for a different paradigm for quality to that which they described as the dominant one. They begin by stating that:

> ... quality in early childhood services is a constructed concept, subjective in nature and based on values, beliefs and interest rather than an objective and universal reality.

They go on to argue that much of the rhetoric of quality has been in the hands of 'powerful stakeholders' such as the university-based researchers and the experts in government. They therefore suggest that 'The approach has been exclusionary in nature and as such has involved the exercise of power and control.' They go on to argue for an inclusive approach that is to be based on:

> … participation by a broad range of stakeholders, and recognition of values, beliefs and interests underpinning definitions. Within this alternative paradigm, the roles, processes and principles typically found within the exclusionary approach are transformed: limited participation is replaced by broad access to the process of definition; power concentration gives way to power distribution; few voices make way for many; an assumption of rational objectivity is challenged by recognition of the essential subjectivity of the process and the role of values, beliefs and interests; the search for quality universals becomes the exchange of quality perspectives leading to definitions specific to a particular spatial and temporal context and capable of evolving through a dynamic and continuous process.

*(Moss and Pence, 1995)*

By 1996, this alternative paradigm could be seen in the definition of quality used in *Quality Targets for Young Children* published by the European Commission Network on Childcare and Other Measures for the Reconciliation of Family and Employment (1996) of which Peter Moss was the Chair:

- quality is a relative concept, based on values and beliefs;
- defining quality is a process and this process is important in its own right, providing opportunities to share, discuss and understand values, ideas, knowledge and experience;
- the process should be participatory and democratic, involving different groups including children, parents and families and professionals working in services;
- the needs, perspectives and values of these groups may sometimes differ;
- defining quality should be seen as a dynamic and continuous process, involving regular review and never reaching a final, 'objective' statement.

*(European Commission, 1996)*

Some would argue that much of this thinking has influenced, albeit implicitly, the creation of the EYD&CPs as a device for the enhancement of locally-driven services for children. But even if this is so, it is only a good start and does not let Partnerships off the hook as far as understanding and defining their own approach.

Consider these two examples illustrating how the application of different approaches may result in very different experiences for children. Both examples are typical of practice in particular types of provision available in England and both offer services for the same ages of children. Both are covered by the same regulations, save for the Section Five early education inspection that only applies to the first example.

### Example 1

At Thomas's they take your child away in a group of other children for an hour, and you don't see what's going on. You're supposed to make polite conversation with the others but all the time you're thinking 'I hope she's not going to pretend she can't talk'. Then all you get is a letter saying she's not suitable.

The Vice-principal says: 'We're not looking for a three-year-old who can already show evidence of reading and writing ability – although if a child spontaneously points out letters or numbers it's noted. We're looking at what their concentration is, what their level of vocabulary is, we're looking for the spark of curiosity, interest level, sociability – which I suppose adds up to teachability'.

*(Dodd, 1998)*

Here we are being given an insight into the selection process for a privately-run (and not inexpensive) nursery school. The approach to quality is designed to appeal to the parents as consumers whose primary concern is for their child to be successful. The school is prepared to test children under the age of three to ensure that, within their own definition of 'teachability', they actively exclude some children. All the parents who apply are willing to put their children through this process although, as we see, some are clearly upset by it. Posing the question 'Which sort of approach to quality is being applied?' it is relatively easy to see that this is:

- non-participative, exclusionary and expert-driven. The school hierarchy is the expert even though it may not be able to determine the different ways in which the child uses language whilst the mother clearly can.
- Using the classification offered by Pfeffer and Coote, there is probably a mix of traditional, scientific, managerial and consumerist approaches here.
- The classification suggested by Williams is less helpful here and it is likely that within the school and its classrooms some of the mechanics of quality control and quality assurance will be deployed.

What seems very clear is that parents will participate in the selection process to the extent that they are willing to pay for the expertise of the school and that they will tend to assume that the beliefs and values of those who run the school will be in keeping with their own. The extent to which there is reliance on a test to determine the nature of the child's own approach to learning is very significant here. So much of the richness of the child's experience is reduced to a few testable dimensions that will almost inevitably miss many of the child's actual interactions. The likelihood is, of course, that all the children who attend this particular school will do well in all subsequent testing in their school careers. It would, however, be unwise to assume that this means that these methods should be universally applied. It is probable that even if every child's family could afford a place, the majority of under-threes in England would fail the selection process. Indeed, one could argue that the school would deem the test to be failing in its part in their quality process if many children did not fail it. One could also argue that, intentionally or not, there is a clear elitist intent in this example.

### Example 2

If the Project is to have an effect on the development of younger children, it must offer an environment where they feel safe, relaxed, and at home, and where they will be stimulated to learn. If children are being stimulated to learn they will be imaginative and creative, they will be expressive, they will explore their environment and make choices for themselves, they will also become more confident, and they will learn new skills.

*(Thomas, 1999)*

Our second example has many of the characteristics of quality that are to be found in the DfEE guidance, as mentioned above. In particular Cynon Valley is:

- focussed on meeting children's needs;
- play, care and education are brought together;
- parents and other family members are involved and there is support for family learning;
- there are very clear criteria which the providers are expected to meet.

Unlike St Thomas's, the Cynon Valley Project is a community development project which started with a vision as follows:

Children were at the heart of the Project's approach that was in fact very straightforward. The theory went something like this: the Project would provide services for pre-school children that would help their development. Parents would bring their children to a children's open access Drop In and stay in the building in an adjacent room where nothing would be expected of them other than to spend time together. Opportunities would however be offered to parents, and they would be supported in planning any activities they wanted to organise. By planning and taking part in new activities together, parents would gain in confidence, knowledge and skills, in other words, they would go through a process of personal development which would lead to empowerment. In time some parents might wish to take over the running of the Project's child care services, or to set up some new activities or groups (not necessarily involving pre-school children). The Project would put parents in a position to keep running the new groups or activities in the longer term. This would allow parents to put their new power to work for the benefit of the community. The end result would be new services and activities, planned and run by local people.

*(Thomas, 1999)*

Subsequently the project began to deliver local training programmes for adults who, in turn, began to run the local services, including the one from which our example derives. Parents/practitioners in setting out their own aspirations for their children are creating their own definition of quality, setting their own standards if you will. However, as this example shows, this need not contradict standards set externally to the settings to which they will be locally applied. It is very unlikely that the approach defined here would in any way be in conflict with the Early Learning Goals or the guidance for these. But the local process is all the more powerful because it meets both the locally-owned definition and complies with national expectations. This is meaningful synergy.

We can also see that the Cynon Valley Project fits with Coote and Pfeffer's 'democratic approach' and the 'inclusive' Moss and Pence model. There is clearly a mixture of total quality and quality assurance occurring locally and we know that external inspection will provide a process of quality control.

What many will find more exciting about Cynon Valley and the other local projects like it, which are increasing in number in the UK, is how they mirror many of the characteristics of the big international exemplars of our time. The Reggio Emilia schools have their own distinct and internationally acclaimed approach that flows from a cluster of locally-owned goals, standards and aspirations:

- the image of the child;
- the expressive arts in the pre-school ;
- progettazione;
- community and parent-school relations;
- environment;
- teachers as learners.

*(Progettazione is notoriously difficult to translate, the term is often understood to mean emergent or child-centred curriculum, but the reality is far more complex. Reggio educators talk of working without a teacher-led curriculum but this does not mean that planning and preparation do not take place. Rather, teachers learn to observe children closely, listen to them carefully and give value to their own ideas so that they might gain an understanding of what interests children most and create strategies that allow the children to build upon their interests.)*

*(Rinaldi, 1998)*

This particular combination relates very closely to the list Jerome Bruner (1999) calls the 'musical themes' of early childhood education and care:

- self-esteem;
- locatedness;
- self-agency;
- culture;
- language;
- play.

And indeed Bruner is nothing less than inspiring when speaking of the Reggio approach:

> … having a sense of place, knowing where you are, somehow helps you develop a sense of your own personal identity, your uniqueness, as well as your place in the world. After my first week, observing Reggio, I was struck by the fact that these were not just 'Reggio Schools', but an expression of a kind of 'Reggiano Spirit'. Every place has its own spirit, its own past, its own aspirations for the future. And this spirit grows out of the ground.
>
> *(Bruner, 1999)*

Many people in England see the Reggio schools as the quintessence of excellence but do not take a lead from home-grown exemplars such as Cynon Valley which reflect the Reggio characteristics. Projects like Cynon Valley are difficult to replicate in the current climate because they require a long lead in time, a ten-year time scale and independent funding. Faced with these realities, Partnerships often opt to have only one exemplary project and not to connect that thinking to broader strategies. Indeed, Early Excellence and Sure Start can be said to be modelling a piecemeal approach. There is also a tendency to replicate only some aspects of Reggio such as the use of the expressive arts but many would argue that Reggio is a whole-system approach or it is nothing.

Reggio educators themselves would argue that attempts to replicate only parts of the approach misrepresent their approach quite profoundly. It is vital to recognise that Reggio is a democratic and inclusionary 'whole village' approach. It is helpfully summed up by *New* as:

> The concept of 'schooling as a system of relations' which guides the work in Reggio Emilia produces much more than good feelings on the part of those involved. This emphasis on relations represents a commitment to engagement in multiple levels of discourse among and between teachers and parents, schools and the larger community. The success with which parents, citizens, and teachers in Reggio Emilia have negotiated their educational aim and processes based on shared understandings of their children provides compelling support for the premise that conceptions of quality and developmental appropriateness cannot be derived from formulaic interpretation of children's development, nor can personal or professional knowledge of children dominate the conversation. Rather, the determination of quality approaches to children's care and education requires a functional system of relations where divergent and minority voices count, with coordinated and collaborative efforts to improve everyone's 'image of the child.' Ongoing documentation of children's learning, advocacy for children's rights, and the participation of all stakeholders-parents (as well as other citizens of the community) will significantly contribute to this process and its outcomes.
>
> *(New, 1998)*

Carlina Rinaldi from Reggio explains this further:

> Participation is an educational strategy that characterises our way of being and teaching. Participation of the children, the teachers and the families, not only by taking part in something but by being part of it, its essence, part of a common identity, a 'we' that we give life to through participation.

*(Rinaldi, 1999)*

The deep significance of Reggio is, therefore, in the support that it offers and the critical understanding that it brings to our own DfEE guidance and implicit approach. The DfEE requires us to use a 'partnership' model that, in the specific interests of quality, they say should 'generate genuine debate between all providers and others, and seek agreement about how those needs can best be met' (DfEE, 1999). *This may therefore mean establishing what is meant locally by partnership and applying this as an educational strategy throughout a commonly-owned quality process or system of relations.*

Does this analysis help our Partnerships and what, apart from the links made above to the partnership model itself, can be concluded about approaches to quality that is of practical value to the EYD&CPs? To start with, it seems to us that Partnerships need to understand that the approach to quality underpinning their strategies and action plans is important. As our examples show, it does make a difference to the eventual experiences of children and therefore it is essential that the approach and the process within which it is embodied are actively chosen and articulated whatever they are. Alternatively, each setting could simply take their lead from the national regulator and differentially interpret their own quality standards, but it is generally accepted that external inspection is insufficient in itself to achieve quality. Nor will this reflect the local characteristics which Reggio (and the DfEE Guidance) show to be so important.

As we shall see, the Integration in Practice Project has demonstrated the wide influence of diverse existing frameworks. What is much less clear is how each local authority and their respective Partnerships have brought all of this thinking into a coherent local process. As we have said, much of the detailed work is not contextualised within the local management or consultation systems, although there is without doubt much which expresses what the authors of the documentation think is lacking in local practice. It is also worth noting that there is little agreement about the use of words: 'approach' and 'process' are almost interchangeable, which is unhelpful. Recent writing and international work suggests that perhaps the use of the concept of quality has outlived its usefulness being either too elusive or inappropriate.

In their new work *Beyond Quality in Early Childhood Education and Care* (Dahlberg, Moss and Pence, 1999), Moss and Pence, this time working with Gunilla Dahlberg, use two concepts to discuss a way forward which goes beyond their previous formulation of a 'inclusionary' paradigm for quality. These are:

**The discourse of quality**
The concept of quality is primarily about defining, through the specification of criteria, a generalizable standard against which a product can be judged with certainty. The process of specification of criteria, and their systematic and methodical application, is intended to enable us to know whether or not something – be it a manufactured or service product – achieves the standard. Central to the construction of quality is the assumption that there is an entity or essence of quality, which is a knowable, objective and certain truth waiting 'out there' to be discovered and described.

**The discourse of meaning making**
In place of talk about programs and projects, we prefer to talk about conjectures and images and contradictions and ambiguities that accompany ideas that we value when we choose our way of life and society. We believe that we will never fully understand and nail down these ideas because their meanings will continue to shift and drift. These are not reasons for despair. It is just the way things are, as we understand them, when we cope with education, society and living. (Cherryholmes, 1994: p. 205)

*(Dahlberg, Moss and Pence, 1999)*

As might be anticipated Dahlberg, Moss and Pence argue strongly that the discourse of meaning-making has more value as a way of thinking about the hugely complex, difficult to define and continuously changing phenomena which are touched on within the DfEE description of the quality principle. The idea of a 'discourse of meaning-making' is very attractive in the early years and childcare worlds and clearly fits what we know happens in our networking systems where we constantly compare and evaluate with each other. This networking can easily be seen as informal benchmarking and thereby easily fitted into the wider systems of organisation and control which constitute government.

However, Michael Schratz, working within an EU funded project 'EVA, a European Pilot Project on quality evaluation in school education' (1998), suggests that it is vital to identify and understand the 'steering options in quality development' and we have been impressed by the following matrix which offers a way of considering local programmes in the terms used above to describe different approaches to quality. In the Schratz matrix we can see, for example, that his 'participation strategy' equates with Coote and Pfeffer's 'democratic approach', and also the locally-driven 'system of relations' at the heart of the Reggio approach. It is self-evident that this also fits with the 'inclusionary paradigm' of Moss and Pence. What we could call the St Thomas's approach is clearly a centralised approach driven by either an external hierarchy or professional self-steering mechanism.

**Figure 1.3    Matrix of steering options in quality development**

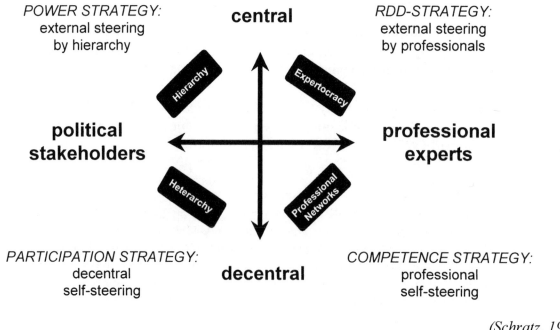

*POWER STRATEGY:*
external steering
by hierarchy

**central**

*RDD-STRATEGY:*
external steering
by professionals

**political
stakeholders**

**professional
experts**

*PARTICIPATION STRATEGY:*
decentral
self-steering

**decentral**

*COMPETENCE STRATEGY:*
professional
self-steering

*(Schratz, 1998)*

Finally, we have considered the following example from the Bernard van Leer Foundation of their *Effectiveness Initiative 1999-2002* which seems to offer a uniquely practical synthesis of much of what the DfEE and the community of UK practitioners are looking for. This investigation is being conducted over a three-year period 'to discover what we can about what makes an effective programme work and to initiate an international dialogue on effectiveness'. Each programme is an Early Childhood Development programme.

The objectives of this investigation were:

- to identify ten diverse Early Childhood Development (ECD) programmes that people consider effective (and that have operated for at least ten years) and to explore them in depth;
- to engage people from the chosen sites, together with staff from international LAGOS, to work in cross-site, cross-cultural teams to carry out such explorations;
- to learn how to apply qualitative research techniques in the examination of ECD programmes;
- to create tools that allow us to understand the complexity of these programme experiences more fully;
- to stimulate cross-site and inter-agency dialogue about what makes ECD programmes effective, how, and for whom;
- to understand the interplay between a programme's process, activities, and outcome;
- to map the contours of effectiveness: defining what makes a programme effective; under what conditions, and for whom; what supports and what hinders a project under particular conditions and in particular contexts; and what these contours tell us about effective programming more generally.

*(Salole, 1999)*

Those working in the project set out their beliefs about effectiveness as a starting point which include that it:

- cannot be defined in terms of a universally accepted truth. There is no single dimension that would make every early childhood programme effective: We are assuming that there are multiple truths and that there is disagreement about what constitutes an effective programme. We are seeking to know where there is agreement in people's experiences and we are trying to understand something of the nature of the disagreements.
- is a fluctuating concept. The effectiveness of an effort changes over time and as a result of changing conditions.
- cannot be placed on a linear scale along which programmes can be ranked from most to least effective.
- resides in an organisation, yet varies within an organisation. Some parts of the organisation may well be much stronger than other parts. Thus, effectiveness is best represented as a profile that is compounded from the cuts and maps.
- takes time to identify and understand. It is not possible to capture an understanding of what constitutes effective ECD programming in a snapshot. It requires living with and experiencing multiple situations that cannot be reduced to a static study of a single point in time. It requires time to recognise how and when something is effective in process and outcomes.
- is the result of experience, and a composite of many experiences.

*(Salole, 1999)*

There seems much that we can learn here about merging the seemingly disparate worlds of meaning-making and quality.

## Conclusion

What this chapter has demonstrated is that the tasks confronting the EYD&CPs are complex, multidimensional and interest-based. If local programmes for quality, as envisaged by the DfEE guidance, are to be brought into meaningful action then several concurrent systems including Best Value will need to be made to work together. This involves the conscious choice, by local partnerships and their respective settings and local authorities, of a distinct approach to quality and the adoption of a process for enactment of this, which is in keeping with it. The following chapters on methodology, findings and examples, which we have identified, provide a unique national platform from which these can be developed.

# 2. Methodology

The Integration in Practice project used a qualitative methodology in its research design. Qualitative research starts from the assumption that people interpret their world, and act according to their own socially constructed meanings. In this sense, the way in which people explain the world determines their actions. The project sought to discover how the notion of quality in integrated services for children is variously understood, defined and aspired to, and to document the consensus as well as the differences apparent across England.

'Integrated' practice was defined as practice combining the education and care of children. Whilst there are some clear case studies of integration in practice, such as the Early Excellence Centres, which have been evaluated by Professor Christine Pascal (Bertram, 1999), the project did not want to replicate this work. We chose not to design a case study approach to the research, for example. Rather, we wanted to explore the wider picture of how integration is understood across England, and by region, in order to get a sense of whether there is a common understanding of the quality issues. We elected to use an analysis of the documentation relating to quality in integrated practice as a means of gathering data about this wider picture.

Through the work of the Early Childhood Unit at the National Children's Bureau we were aware of the range of materials developed by agencies across the country as tools for quality. The legislative separation of care and education in England has meant that many of these materials are not presented as 'integrated'. They have often been designed to interpret national legislation and guidance and to offer support to practitioners in their implementation. Materials developed for daycare under the Children Act 1989 look specifically at care issues, for example, whilst those dealing with the Qualification and Curriculum Authority's Desirable Learning Outcomes (QCA's DLOs), otherwise known as the Early Learning Goals, focus on education. However, many settings, particularly those catering for three- and four-year-olds in the private and voluntary sectors would typically use both sets of materials to meet both sets of regulator's requirements. It was not expected that there were many materials that would be truly 'integrated'. At the research design stage, it was decided that an audit of materials would need to combine care materials with education materials as well as any integrated materials, to bring together the different elements of quality and give an overall picture of what integration looks like in practice. Materials were therefore requested from:

- Early Years Development and Childcare Partnerships: plans, audits and other documents, in particular kitemark schemes where they existed;
- Registration and Inspection Units: daycare guidance;
- Local Education Authorities: curriculum guidance and other materials relating to education.

In addition, materials developed by national organisations and the academic sector known to be widely used in the field, were also requested. Amongst these were:

- Aiming High (Kids' Clubs Network, 1996)
- The Effective Early Learning Project (Pascal, 1994)
- Aiming for Quality (Pre-School Learning Alliance, 1996)
- Quality in Diversity (Early Childhood Education Forum, 1998)

The major shortcoming of an audit like this on its own is that the status of the documents was not always clear. Many documents audited, for example, were not dated and may not have been current. Often there was no acknowledgment of the ownership of documents, the extent to which they were used or the means of application. There was no means of discerning whether the materials were thoroughly used and implemented in all settings and with all age groups across a local authority area, or were developed by education advisers for use in schools, for example. There was little acknowledgment of key reference points or influences on the authors of the documents. The audit also does not take into account any integrated standards, which might be developed at setting level, since with the exception of one Early Excellence Centre, these materials were not sent for audit.

The project also noted that some materials seemed to be heavily weighted in one particular area, and developed the notion of the 'deficit' model of quality development. This described the process whereby the group of people writing a specific set of materials would agree that they were concerned about the lack of good practice in a particular area, and weight the materials to support development in this area. One set of curriculum guidance, for example, emphasised 'sand' in every learning area, giving the impression that activities with sand alone would support all children's learning. Following this up, it transpired that many of the settings in this rural county were using multi-use community premises. The village hall committees who had just raised the money to revarnish the floor did not appreciate sand and neither did the aerobics class which used the hall in the evening. It looked as if the authors of the materials had simply wanted to encourage providers not to abandon the idea of sand, and to reinforce its importance in children's learning.

Some of these shortcomings are in the nature of quality development. The same group of people who developed one set of materials in 1998, for example, would no doubt develop a very different set of materials in 2000. They would have developed their own thinking during that period, no doubt have been influenced by new research findings and a professional development visit to a renowned centre of excellence in the UK or abroad, the legislative context changed in that period and there would be new concerns about local practice. Quality is a dynamic concept, and it is right that it should change over time.

What is perhaps more important is the issue of bias here. The people who developed the documents, would, in most cases, be local authority employees, external consultants, acknowledged 'experts' at a high level in their organisation. The HERA 2 project has documented, through its research into the workforce (Cordeaux, 1999), the mismatch between the views of the workforce in the private and voluntary sectors about quality in childcare and those of the 'experts'. The extent to which the views and aspirations within the materials audited were shared by the workforce as a whole is questionable.

May (1993) discusses the problems of viewing documents as reporting social reality, and advocates that the researcher should examine the process of the production of a document as well as the social and political context in which it has been written. Documents 'do not simply reflect, but also construct social reality and versions of events ... documents are now viewed as mediums through which social power is expressed.' In many cases, the processes by which a document had been produced were unclear. Some had clearly been written by consortia of 'experts', others by single authors, still others through a consultative process. In most cases, not enough information was available in the documents themselves to ascertain their authorship. The research findings therefore cannot assume that the documents are representative of the views of all stakeholders in a local authority area. On the other hand, the status of the documents is clearer. They have been openly published by the local authority or agency concerned for public use and therefore carry an official sanction. Whilst this cannot be taken to mean that the content of the documents represents the reality of practice, it can be assumed that they are a significant influence on practice.

Scott (1990) suggests four criteria for assessing documents for research purposes: authenticity; credibility; representativeness; and meaning. In the case of the Integration in Practice Project, the documents used are both authentic and credible in that they have official recognition and to that extent they are representative of their genre. The issue of meaning is more complex. Scott defined meaning as being constructed through what the author(s) intended, the meaning given to it by the intended audience and the actual content of the text. The task of the researcher in this exercise is, therefore, not only to undertake a thorough text analysis of the content of the document, but also to apply an understanding of the social and political context in which it has been written and what the author(s) hoped to achieve through its publication. As participants in this same social world, with knowledge of the sector, we also used our own understanding to interpret the meanings, which an intended audience might have given to them.

To test the validity of the findings of the audit, and explore their meanings in more depth, as well as to gain another source of data, the project also held two focus groups in each region and a meeting of national coordinators and registration and inspection staff. The regional focus groups were held at the initial stage of the data collection to explain the project and to gain a first response to the idea of quality in integration. These were useful sources in terms of orientating the interpretation of the data. The second focus group in each region took place after data analysis at regional level, and served as a means of testing the validity of the findings and helping to refine the development of categories. The regional groups were also able to help to explain regional differences in the data. The majority of these groups comprised local authority coordinators either from education or social services, who were often employed as officers to the Early Years Development and Childcare Partnerships. Although attendance varied, a minimum of 20 people attended regional focus groups and over 70 people attended the national meeting.

Qualitative research allows for the fact that the researcher is also part of the social world, and can be included not only within the research focus, but can also be used to develop and test theory. Both researchers were familiar with the early years field through both practice and research experience, and therefore had a sense of the 'foreshadowed problems' (Malinowski, 1922). We expected to find elements of quality as defined through the key policy and legislative drivers such as:

- Children Act 1989 (Statutes 1989);
- Qualification and Curriculum Authority's Desirable Learning Outcomes (now Early Learning Goals) (QCA 1999a);
- National Childcare Strategy

We also expected to find influences of key early years theories such as those put forward by High/Scope and Montessori Education, as well as international influences from Reggio Emilia in Italy, for example, and we anticipated that there would be local influences on definitions of quality. We used these 'hunches' to explain the project to participants in the focus groups from the outset, and later to help us understand the data we collected.

As with most qualitative research, the analysis of data is not a distinct stage of the research, but continues through data collection and the writing up of the research and feeds into the research design. The project used the idea of 'grounded theorizing' (Glaser and Strauss, 1967) whereby 'the collection of data is guided strategically by the developing theory. Theory building and data collection are dialectically linked'. The reflexivity in relationship between analysis, data collection and research design enables a constant testing of the developing theory.

As the project developed, there were significant national initiatives, which influenced its focus. The project originally aimed to look at the issue of quality of integrated practice for children from birth to eight-year-olds in line with Children Act 1989 guidance on Daycare. The National Childcare Strategy however, had a focus on children aged from birth to 14-year-olds, and quality of services across this age range was a concern for the Early Years Development and Childcare Partnerships. It was agreed with the Department for Education and Employment that the age range should be extended to children from birth to age 14. The development of the Care Standards Bill, and the new Daycare Standards within it, embracing both care and education of children, has also been an important influence. In the latter stages of the project, data has been analysed to test the emerging draft standards. The policy context has influenced the breadth of the research and the way in which it has been presented, and the project has been keen to ensure that its findings informed policy development where possible.

In order to gain access to the types of materials outlined above, requests were sent to national organisations with known quality programmes and locally to the Regional Local Authority Coordinators' Network. The Coordinators' Network combines key staff in the early years sector from each of the local authorities in England and meets regularly on a regional basis. The network is maintained by the Early Childhood Unit at the National Children's Bureau. The initial requests to coordinators were followed up with specific requests to Registration and Inspection Units where Daycare Guidance had not been automatically sent. The process of data collection took place between July 1999 and February 2000 on a region by region basis. Feedback was given to two regions in September 1999, to three more regions in November and December 1999 and to the final four regions between January and March 2000. This timetable enabled a constant analysis of data. Whilst the data collection process focussed on the regional timetable, a final analysis combining all data, including that from regions which had sent in materials after their regional feedback, was completed in March 2000.

The Local Authority Early Years Coordinators' Network served as an excellent means of collecting documents. The project was presented at an initial meeting, and subsequent meetings reminded coordinators to send in materials. In addition, coordinators from areas with low representation were followed up through telephone calls.

The response rate was extremely good, as can be seen by Table 2.1 below.

**Table 2.1    Response rate by region**

| Local Authorities by Region | % response rate |
|---|---|
| London | 55 |
| East | 70 |
| Yorkshire and the Humber | 75 |
| West Midlands | 80 |
| East Midlands | 100 |
| South West | 65 |
| North East | 60 |
| North West | 31 |
| South East | 75 |

With the exception of the North West, the response rate was well over 50 per cent – a national average of 68 per cent.

There were 290 documents collected over the project period. Twenty documents came from national and international sources and 268 from regional sources. The breakdown of materials by national/international category, region and by type is shown in the tables below:

**Table 2.2    National and international materials**

| Organisation | Material |
|---|---|
| Effective Early Learning (EEL) | Effective Early Learning project (Pascal, Bertram and Ramdsden, 1994) |
| Goldsmiths College | Principles into Practice project, Goldsmiths College (Blenkin & Kelly, 1997) |
| High/Scope | High/Scope approach to the National Curriculum (Brown, 1990) |
| Holtermann 1992 | Holterman, S. Investing in young children (Holterman, 1992/1995) |
| Investors in People | |
| Kids' Clubs Network | Aiming High (KCN, 1996) |
| Montessori Education (UK) | Montessori Curriculum (Montessori, 1995) |
| National Childminding Association | Children Come First (1998) |
| National Day Nurseries Association | Quality Assurance (1999) |
| Out of school care: Federation of the Highlands and Islands | Good Practice Guide for Out of School Care Projects (Federation, 1999) |
| Pre school Learning Alliance | Aiming For Quality (PLA, 1996) |
| PQASSO | Practical quality assurance system for small organisations (Charities Evaluation Services, 1997) |
| Qualifications and Curriculum Authority | Baseline Assessment (QCA, 1998) |
| Qualifications and Curriculum Authority | Desirable Learning Outcomes (QCA, 1996) |
| Qualifications and Curriculum Authority | Early Learning Goals (QCA, 1999a) |
| Qualifications and Curriculum Authority | Review Of Desirable Learning Outcomes (QCA, 1999b) |
| Early Childhood Education Forum | Quality in Diversity (1998) |
| RSA 1994 | Start Right Report (Ball, 1994) |
| UN Convention | United Nations Convention on the Rights of the Child (UN, 1991) |
| University of Glasgow | Evaluating Ourselves (Wilkinson & Stephen, 1992) |

**Table 2.3      Regional documents**

| Region | No. of documents | Integrated | Education | R&I | EYD&CP | Training | Other |
|---|---|---|---|---|---|---|---|
| London | 60 | 10 | 14 | 12 | 12 | 2 | 10 |
| East | 13 | 1 | 4 | | 5 | | 3 |
| Yorkshire and Humberside | 32 | 6 | 10 | 10 | 6 | | |
| West Midlands | 28 | 4 | 10 | 3 | 4 | 1 | 6 |
| East Midlands | 24 | 2 | 4 | 9 | 6 | | 3 |
| South West | 21 | 5 | 5 | 5 | 5 | 1 | |
| North East | 26 | | 5 | 9 | 4 | 4 | 4 |
| North West | 18 | | 8 | 1 | 3 | 1 | 5 |
| South East | 46 | 6 | 6 | 16 | 13 | 1 | 4 |
| Total | 268 | 34 | 66 | 65 | 58 | 10 | 35 |
| % | | 12.7 | 24.6 | 24.3 | 21.6 | 3.7 | 13.1 |

The data collected has almost equal representation of care (Registration and Inspection: R&I above) and education materials and almost a quarter of the materials were from Early Years Development and Childcare Partnerships. Education materials mostly focussed on three- to five-year-olds, Registration and Inspection materials on from birth to eight-year-olds and Early Years Development and Childcare Partnership materials on from birth to age fourteen.

Recording and organising data from such a wide range of materials, which were often produced in different styles and for different audiences, required careful management. Some of the documents were weighty files, and in order to make comparisons, it was necessary to summarise the data. This enabled us to cover the large amount of information available, however, some of that information was necessarily lost and we needed to decide which were the important points and start to translate them into categories in order to make the summary. This meant that we had to introduce interpretation at a fairly early stage. However, to minimise our own bias in this exercise and so as to lose as little as possible of the detail, we chose to develop a wide range of categories and subcategories at the start of the research process. By the time we had analysed two regions, we had developed 471 different subcategories.

At the start we categorised the materials by the way in which they presented, that is, materials that described:

- evaluation frameworks;
- what children should learn about;
- how children learn;
- the adult role;
- outcomes of approaches;
- values and underpinning principles.

While some materials had elements of all of these and would be categorised in all six areas, some would appear in only a few. Each of these categories then had subcategories.

We used Microsoft Excel spreadsheets to store and retrieve the data. At the start of the project we were using three different spreadsheets combining the six areas above in order to hold the numbers of subcategories that were being developed.

Whilst this was an effective way of describing the materials, it did not help when we started to undertake the first regional analysis. There was too wide a range of data to make sense of. It was at this stage that we started the process of what Hammersley and Atkinson (1983) call 'progressive focusing', where we tried to encompass the breadth of the data whilst grouping it into more manageable categories. In order to do so, we placed all the subcategories from the six areas above side by side and combined them.

We used the project steering group, made up of experts from a range of sectors in the field, to help us in this task. For example 'access' issues appeared in nearly all categories several times, either under 'access to information', 'rural access' or accessibility in general. These categories were then combined into a single category named 'access'. Table 2.4 below shows the combination of subcategories that create the category 'autonomy', for example.

**Table 2.4    Combination of subcategories, which create the category 'autonomy'**

| Spreadsheet 1: evaluation frameworks | Spreadsheet 2: learning (what and how), adult role and outcomes | Spreadsheet 3: values and underpinning principles | Number of mentions | Final category |
|---|---|---|---|---|
| Autonomy | | | 2 | Autonomy |
| | Autonomy | | 14 | Autonomy |
| | | Children who are decision-makers/problem-solvers | 5 | Autonomy |
| | | Choice/motivation | 2 | Autonomy |
| | Critical thinking | | 4 | Autonomy |
| | Decision-making | | 9 | Autonomy |
| | Generating new strategies | | 2 | Autonomy |
| | How decisions impact on others | | 2 | Autonomy |
| | Independence | | 1 | Autonomy |
| | | Independence | 5 | Autonomy |
| | Own lives | | 1 | Autonomy |
| | Plan – Do – Review | | 3 | Autonomy |
| | Problem-solving approach | | 8 | Autonomy |
| | Reflection | | 5 | Autonomy |
| | | Reflective children | 4 | Autonomy |
| | Responsibility | | 1 | Autonomy |
| | | Responsibility | 2 | Autonomy |
| | Setting problems/challenges | | 5 | Autonomy |
| | Share control, enable children to make choices | | 4 | Autonomy |
| | Taking care of own needs | | 2 | Autonomy |

From the table above it is clear that there are a range of possible meanings for the category 'autonomy' and a range of ways in which they can be used in practice. The concept of autonomy can be part of an evaluation framework, an underpinning belief about the way in which work with children should be approached, something that children should develop as a skill, and a teaching strategy. Most materials tend to talk about autonomy in relation to teaching and learning strategies and it is not commonly used as part of evaluation frameworks. The use of spreadsheets to store and retrieve data enabled us not only to keep the breadth of the data, examine patterns of meaning and how they were used, but also to organise it into more manageable formats. At the end of this first attempt at analysis, 62 categories had been agreed, which we called 'Quality Areas'.

Once this had been done, the three spreadsheets were amalgamated into one with the 62 categories heading up each column, and all subsequent data was matched to these categories and new ones created if necessary.

The process of data collection, as has already been mentioned was, in effect, done in three stages. The first set of data to be collected and analysed were the national materials and materials from the Eastern region and Yorkshire and the Humber. Our initial analysis used only these findings. Our second analysis took place in November 1999 to enable feedback to London, and East and West Midlands, the third in January 2000 before feedback sessions to South East, South West, North East and North West regions. A final analysis of all data took place in March 2000.

As data was collected and stored, some new Quality Areas emerged initially, and, as a result of the focus group discussions at feedback sessions, some Quality Areas were combined. By the third stage of data collection, all data was accommodated within the Quality Areas, giving us some confidence that we had reached 'saturation point'. Theoretical saturation is the term used by Glaser and Strauss (1967) to mean the point in qualitative research where data does not modify or question the categories developed, thus indicating the end of that phase of the research. Table 2.5 shows the progress of the Quality Areas over the first three stages of analysis.

**Table 2.5    Progress of the Quality Areas**

|   | Quality Area: Stage 1 | Quality Area: Stage 2 | Quality Area: Stage 3 |
|---|---|---|---|
| 1 | Access | Access: to provision, within provision, resources for all | Access |
| 2 | Active learning | Active learning: through first hand experience | Administration |
| 3 | Activities | Activities | Admissions and transition |
| 4 | Administration | Administration | Affordable |
| 5 | Admissions and transitions | Administration | Aims and objectives |
| 6 | Affordable | Affordable provision | Atmosphere: ethos, how it 'feels' |
| 7 | Aims and objectives | Aims and objectives | Behaviour: policy, expectations |
| 8 | Alone | Alone: children working alone | Best value |
| 9 | Atmosphere | Atmosphere: ethos | Child protection |
| 10 | Autonomy: children solving problems, making decisions, taking responsibility, adults sharing control | Autonomy | Children's rights |
| 11 | Behaviour; policy, expectations | Behaviour | Communication |
| 12 | Building on learning | Building on learning | Complaints |
| 13 | Child protection | Child Protection | Confidentiality |
| 14 | Children's rights | Children's rights | Continuity |
| 15 | Communication | Communication | Developmental age and stage: appropriate activities |
| 16 | Community involvement | Community involvement | Dlos (6 areas) |
| 17 | Complaints | Complaints | Environment: layout, safety, maintenance, use of space |
| 18 | Confidentiality | Confidentiality | Equal opportunities: anti-discrimination, multi-cultural practice, policy, access |
| 19 | Continuity | Consultation: with children and adults | Equipment: maintenance, safety |

| | | | |
|---|---|---|---|
| 20 | Desirable learning outcomes | Continuity | Food: preparation of, times of |
| 21 | Developmental age and stage: appropriate practice | Developmental age and stage: recognition of, appropriate provision | Health |
| 22 | Environment | Desirable Learning Outcomes (Early Learning Goals) | Health and safety |
| 23 | Equal opportunities | Employment: parents, employers, links with services | HIV/Aids |
| 24 | Equipment: maintenance and safety | Environment: layout, organisation, indoor and outdoor, display | Insurance |
| 25 | Food | Equal opportunities: equal concern, anti-discriminatory practice, multi-cultural awareness and resources, languages other than English | Integrated |
| 26 | Group | Equipment: maintenance, diversity | Learning and teaching strategies, Alone: opportunities for children to work/play alone, Autonomy: includes children solving problems, making decisions, taking responsibility, adults sharing control, Building on learning, Group: opportunities for children to work/play in groups, Time and space: for children's learning at own place, Active learning |
| 27 | Health | Family support | Learning experiences |
| 28 | Health and safety | Flexibility | Lifelong learning |
| 29 | HIV/Aids | Food: social aspect of mealtimes, nutrition, reflect cultural diversity, hygiene | Management: resource, financial, staff, adequate structures |
| 30 | Insurance | Group: children working as a group | Marketing: dissemination, advertising |
| 31 | Integrated provision | Health | Monitoring and evaluation |
| 32 | Learning and teaching strategies | Health and safety | Observation and assessment |
| 33 | Learning experiences | HIV/Aids | Outings and transport: procedures, safety |
| 34 | Lifelong learning | Information: provision of | Parent partnership: including sharing information two-way, parenting support, prime educators of children, reflecting culture |
| 35 | Management | Insurance | Partnership; working with other agencies/cross-sector, Community involvement: area planning, liaison with other settings, professionals, reflecting community in planning |
| 36 | Marketing: dissemination, advertising | Integrated provision | Planning: all areas |
| 37 | Monitoring and evaluation | Interagency/cross-sector partnership | Play |
| 38 | Observation and assessment | Learning and teaching strategies | Policies in place |
| 39 | Outings and transport: procedures, safety | Learning experiences | Professional development: reflective practice, training and qualifications, supervision and appraisals |
| 40 | Parent partnership | Lifelong learning | Quality assurance |
| 41 | Partnership: working with other agencies/cross-sector | Management | Range of provision: choice |
| 42 | Planning | Marketing: dissemination of good practice | Records: keeping records |
| 43 | Play | Monitoring and evaluation | Reflective children |
| 44 | Policies in place | Observation and assessment | Regeneration: participating in economic development/area planning strategies |
| 45 | Process (not product) | Outings and transport: safety, as part of curriculum | Registered |
| 46 | Professional development | Parent partnership | Relationships: with adults and children and between children |
| 47 | Quality assurance | Planning | Resources: use of, diversity, maintenance |
| 48 | Range of provision: choice | Play | Role model: adult role |
| 49 | Records-keeping | Policies in place | Routine |
| 50 | Reflective children | Process (not product) | Safe and secure |
| 51 | Regeneration: participating in economic development, area planning | Professional development; training, qualifications, reflective practice | Self-esteem: value identity, build confidence |
| 52 | Registered | Quality assurance | SEN: code of practice, access |
| 53 | Relationships | Range/choice of provision | Setting-specific: standards for different settings/occupational groups |
| 54 | Resources | Record-keeping | Staffing: including employment, ratios, meetings, fit persons |
| 55 | Role model: adult role | Reflective children | Target in need: strategic planning |
| 56 | Routine | Regeneration; links to other developments | |
| 57 | Safe and secure | Registered provision | |

| 58 | Self-esteem | Relationships: with adults, children and between children | |
| 59 | SEN: code of practice, access | Resources: diversity of, suitability, safety aspect | |
| 60 | Setting-specific: standards for different settings/occupational groups | Role model (adult role) | |
| 61 | Staffing | Routine | |
| 62 | Target in need: strategic planning | Safe and secure: warm, caring | |
| 63 | Time and space: for children's learning at own pace | Self-esteem: confidence | |
| 64 | | SEN: assessment, provision | |
| 65 | | Setting-specific: age-range | |
| 66 | | Social inclusion: cohesion | |
| 67 | | Staffing: recruitment, supervision, ratios, meetings | |
| 68 | | Sustain and increase provision | |
| 69 | | Target children/communities in need | |
| 70 | | Time and space to learn | |
| 71 | | Best value/efficiency: value for money | |

It is clear that the focus shifted slightly over the period of analysis, and moved from 55 to 71 Quality Areas. Some of these were new areas, but many were combined in response to focus group discussion.

We took this to indicate that the audit had covered the breadth of what integration into practice might mean, although the way in which the Quality Areas might be organised into a smaller number of groupings was more complex.

At each stage of the analysis, all the data was aggregated to give, as far as possible, a total picture of common patterns, but also disaggregated by region (the national materials being counted as being from a 'region' for this purpose) to enable comparison between regions and against the overall picture. The data was stored as excerpts of text or page reference numbers in the Excel spreadsheet, and in order to explore the patterns of emphasis for each particular area by region and as a total, we calculated the 'frequency of mention' to give a weighting to that Quality Area.

Each time a mention was made in a document of a particular Quality Area, a page reference, text or series of references were placed in the column relating to that area. There could only be one possible mention for an area from each document. The frequencies were added up and calculated as an overall percentage (by the total number of documents), or as a regional percentage (by the total number of regional documents received). This gave us a means of comparing regional and national data against each other and against the overall total. The findings demonstrated the emphasis given to particular areas by region and the extent to which Quality Areas were rated in importance both regionally and across England.

An extract from the spreadsheet illustrates some of the findings:

**Table 2.6**      **Frequency of mention (%)**

|  | Access | Family support | Planning | Learning experiences |
|---|---|---|---|---|
| **All areas** | 23.8 | 7.2 | 32.8 | 42.4 |
| **West Midlands** | 25 | 21.4 | 25 | 39.3 |
| **East Midlands** | 20.8 | 4.1 | 20.8 | 25 |
| **London** | 21.6 | 11.6 | 35 | 40 |
| **National** | 4.5 | 0 | 31.8 | 72.7 |
| **Eastern** | 15.3 | 23 | 38.4 | 53.8 |
| **Yorks. and Humber** | 18.8 | 3.1 | 46.9 | 56.2 |
| **South East** | 37 | 0 | 32.6 | 32.6 |
| **South West** | 47.6 | 14.3 | 28.6 | 52.4 |
| **North East** | 15.4 | 0 | 30.1 | 23.1 |
| **North West** | 22.2 | 0 | 38.9 | 22.2 |

Findings are discussed in more detail in the next chapter.

At each feedback session, regional findings were fed back to the region in question, together with the national picture. The national picture changed as did its relationship to the regional data over the project period. The final weightings were calculated in March 2000.

As previously mentioned, the regional focus groups were used as a source of data, and a means of supporting the 'funneling' or progressive focusing work. At the same time the project was keen to ensure the involvement of participants in the development of the research. This was important for the research as a means of validating the data and a method of triangulation, but also important from an ethical perspective.

The Early Childhood Unit has developed a close relationship with the local authority coordinators through its network, and sees its role as not only supporting and working with local partnerships in the sector to help them develop and implement good practice, but also to work closely with policy-makers at a national level to ensure a dialogue between national government and local actors. This 'bottom-up/top-down' facilitation approach has underpinned the work of the Integration in Practice Project. We wanted to implement as participative approach to the research as possible.

The initial focus group session was organised to give an outline of the project and the kinds of influences – statutory, theoretical and local – that underpin the notion of integration. There was then a facilitated discussion on the nature of materials present in each local authority represented at the group and their relationship to integration as well as their currency, status and relevancy to the project. The 'feedback' focus group was presented with the findings of the project thus far, in terms of the Quality Areas and the way in which these were owned across the country, in national materials and in the materials of the region being audited (calculated through the frequency of mention). There was some discussion in general about the findings and then an exercise considering the areas of quality in terms of relevance, which respondents participated in individually and as a group. In later focus groups, respondents also commented on the way in which these areas could be clustered into smaller groups.

Hammersley and Atkinson (1995) warn of the dangers of relying on respondent validation in qualitative research. They point to the fact that, although respondents are good informants of their own actions, they may not be aware of their practice in a particular context, nor may they be able to recognise it when it is documented. Moreover, when research findings are presented to respondents, their reactions may be influenced by other factors than the research itself. We decided deliberately to concentrate on the areas of emphasis in each region, rather than to present areas of comparatively little emphasis, in order not to give the impression that the research was aiming to criticise practice. Regions had the opportunity to look at overall Quality Areas and comment on these in a separate exercise. In this case, focus groups were not always particularly interested in looking at their own regional findings, but were more keen to get involved in exercises discussing the overall Quality Areas and the aspirational aspect of integration into practice and where such a framework would fit within the policy context. This in itself was useful data in terms of helping to refine the Quality Areas.

In some cases the regions recognised themselves in the regional picture of the data, in other cases, they were not so sure, but there was little dispute about the overall Quality Areas as being the concepts which they would expect to see in integrated practice. Focus groups did not appear to think that their regional emphases were in any way incompatible with a broader framework. In this sense, the focus groups provided a useful source of triangulation for the theory that there is a shared sense of the aspirations for integration into current practice, despite any regional differences.

The final 'funneling' exercise took place in March 2000 with the aim of reducing the Quality Areas to seven or eight on the basis that these were more easily retained than 60 or 70. It was clear from the focus groups – few of whom suggested the same sets of clusters – that the exercise would produce a set of clusters that would necessarily be in some way artificial, since another group of people would doubtless have produced another set of equally valid clusters. Indeed, one local authority had already done so. In recognition of this, we agreed to call these clusters 'Organising Principles', acknowledging the fact that we were simply looking at a manageable way of organising the Quality Areas, which, we felt, were not in dispute.

It was at this point that the policy context intervened significantly in the project. The national draft standards for daycare were being produced and it was not possible to consider the Organising Principles in isolation from the 14 draft national standards. The analysis took place in two stages. On the first occasion, the project steering group undertook a content analysis on the text that had been stored under each Quality Area, to look at possible combinations and links between areas. The group was able to agree eight Organising Principles, the majority of which linked directly to one principle. Some Quality Areas were split between different Organising Principles. For example, 'communication' linked to Community Partnership (including parent partnership) where it referred to the need for good communication skills with parents and other agencies, to Learning and Teaching, where it related directly to children's learning and to Staffing and Professional development where it related to work within the team.

Once that exercise had been carried out, a similar analysis was carried out between the Integration into Practice research data and the text in the draft national standards. There was significant commonality between both sets of text with some mismatches, and a slightly differently selected arrangement of the Quality Areas. For example, the Integration into Practice Project had placed 'relationships' within its organising principle Developing Citizenship including other areas such as behaviour, children's rights and self-esteem, whilst the draft national standards had placed it in Care and Learning (the Integration into Practice Learning and Teaching category). The resulting comparison was presented to a national group of over 70 local authority coordinators from across England.

Feedback from this group shows that the Organising Principles could be further refined, and need clearer explanation. The next stage of this project – Quality in Practice – will take this work forward.

Once research findings are in the public domain, political circumstances take over. At the time of writing, the Department for Education and Employment has produced 14 draft national standards for daycare. These will then be put out to national consultation. As we have outlined before, our ethical intention in carrying out this research had been to reach, through evidence of current practice and aspirations to improving practice, a better collective understanding of what is going on in terms of integration in practice, both to inform practice and support local initiatives as well as to contribute to developing national policy. In the last weeks of the project it has been necessary to relate our research to both the draft national standards work at the DfEE and the emerging role of OFSTED. In effect, this is an issue of presentation, not of a change in the research findings.

Writing up qualitative research is a complex process. There are many different ways of presenting research data. Indeed, the process of writing up in itself leads to new reflections on what has been learned during the research project. In writing up this research, it has become clear that the findings represent, not necessarily what is happening across England in terms of integrated practice – although, in some settings, this may be true – but rather what the national and regional stakeholders who hold most influence commonly aspire to. In our view, this is an important perspective to have access to at a time when the regulatory system for this sector is being integrated as well as for continuous improvement strategies.

# 3.    Findings

This chapter will deal with the findings of the Integration in Practice project. As the previous chapter indicated, findings have been organised in a variety of different ways to suit different audiences in project feedback focus groups and in feeding back to national policy-makers. This chapter will outline the Quality Areas and their meanings, the patterns of emphasis overall and by region and the areas of consensus and difference. It will explain the meanings that lie behind the eight Organising Principles and the evidence for support for these across the country and will relate both the Quality Areas and the Organising Principles to the national draft standards for daycare. It will also make reference to the themes and issues raised by the focus groups over the course of the project.

The findings indicate the current state of play in regional and national thinking about integration as it occurs in practice and its quality indicators. They show the range of interpretations of what integration might look like and provide national and local policy-makers with a position statement on quality, at a critical point in the evolution of services for children from birth to age fourteen.

## The Common Quality Areas

The previous chapter demonstrated how the definitions of the Quality Areas changed over the project's lifetime. At the final analysis, we had a working total of 69 Common Quality Areas as outlined in the table below. The meanings summarised in this table are taken from the various texts of the materials that were audited. They would not necessarily be suitable for all settings or all types of providers. Many of them would need to be reworked specifically to include the context in which childminders work, for example. The summaries are intended to give an indication of the range of meanings and understandings covered by the concept of 'Quality Area'. The summaries are not necessarily coherent in themselves, and sometimes contradict each other. The meanings below should not therefore be read as definitions, but as an indication of the *range* of meanings covered in each of the Common Quality Areas. The areas which predominate are shown later in this chapter.

## Table 3.1    69 Common Quality Areas

| 69 Common Quality Areas | Meaning |
|---|---|
| ACCESS | PARENTS: in rural areas, to local provision. Flexible attendance. Subsidies and flexibility on fees.<br>PROVIDERS: Monitor access to provision to ensure equality of access. Access to written policies for parents.<br>CHILDREN: Accessible equipment and curriculum for children. To training and support for providers. Disability access for children and adults. Access for children of all ages and abilities, children in need, minority ethnic groups, travellers, refugees, bilingual children, and homeless families. |
| ACTIVE LEARNING | Children learn most effectively when actively involved and interested. **Children should be involved in planning and be facilitated to learn through first hand experience rather than by being told.** Staff should encourage active involvement. |
| ACTIVITIES | A wide variety of activities should be available, regularly planned and reviewed with children and with clear learning objectives. Activities should promote physical, cognitive and social skills and be relevant and enjoyable. Programmes should include imaginative and adventurous activities that care for the environment, oneself as an individual and others in the community. They should be multi-cultural, multi-ethnic, reflective of home environment, freely chosen, self-correcting, graded in difficulty, link to real life and real purpose and always available. Activities can include: visits/trips, junk, recycling, markmaking, woodwork, cutting, stocking, sewing, joining, IT, small world, books and tapes, storytelling, caring for living things, paint, food processing, music, sound, dance, role play, water, games and puzzles, outdoor, bricks and blocks, natural objects, seasons, celebrations, themes. Children should be involved in planning and programmes discussed with parents. Activities should be accessible to children with physical, sensory and/or learning disabilities. A daily/weekly programme should be planned. |
| ADMINISTRATION | Settings should keep records on children's details, register of attendance, accident books and staff, and ensure confidentiality. There should be a constitution, notes of important decisions, an annual report and financial accounts. Plans should be kept and reviewed and used for staff development plans. Policies and procedures should be known by staff and monitored. There should be written contracts with parents that are regularly reviewed. Hours of work should be agreed and reviewed and notice and holiday arrangements clarified and staff enabled to take religious holidays. Finance systems should be maintained and records of users, staff and volunteers. Documentary evidence of operations should be maintained for evaluation purposes. Waiting lists should be maintained, and staff ratios ensured. The relationship with the Early Years Development and Childcare Partnership should be maintained. |
| ADMISSIONS and TRANSITIONS | Work and plan with other providers including sharing of records, to ensure gradual, smooth transition. **Admissions policy should be clear and issues such as routine of the child, routine of the group, expectations, payment and hours, holiday and sickness, bringing and collecting and settling in procedures clarified with parents at outset.** |
| AFFORDABILITY | Settings should provide value for money, be cost-effective, and affordable for the target group. Employers can support settings and other funding streams can be used. |

| AIMS and OBJECTIVES | **Underpinning values should be clearly stated and shared**. These could include: appropriate curriculum, equal opportunities, respecting children as individuals, ensuring minority ethnic groups are valued within the setting, safe, challenging, stimulating, caring, sharing environment, lifelong access to quality education, contributing to economic and cultural development, integrated view of child development, promoting equality, working in partnership, open and accessible, empowerment of the sector, commitment to the highest quality, children come first, community support, consistent service, integrated service, inclusion of children with special needs. These values should be evident through policies and reflected in the view of parents and children. |
| --- | --- |
| ALONE | **Children should have the opportunity to learn individually with and without an adult.** |
| ATMOSPHERE | Settings should have a bright, friendly, positive, welcoming atmosphere where children and families are valued and respected and where children are treated holistically and encouraged and praised. Settings should recognise the child's needs and celebrate success. There should be a sense of belonging where children feel confident and comfortable and secure. Positive image should be encouraged as respect for all. There should be a shared commitment by all stakeholders to this positive ethos. Care and education should be integrated. |
| AUTONOMY | Children make decisions, take responsibility, solve problems, take risks, develop self-help skills, direct their own learning, plan, initiate and reflect on their work. Adults share control, encourage independence and empower children. Opportunities should be available for children to make choices, work independently, tidy up after themselves, and develop the confidence to be independent. |
| BEHAVIOUR | There should be positive expectations of children's behaviour with clear rules and boundaries consistently applied. A behaviour policy should include no smacking, shaking, slapping, humiliation, bullying and parents should be kept informed. Intervention should be appropriate to the developmental stage of the child. Good behaviour should be rewarded, encouraged and praised. **The child should not be criticised, only for any unacceptable behaviour.** There should be sympathetic treatment of any sleep and toilet-training problems. Behaviour support plans can be used, behaviour monitored, and appropriate sanctions used. Adults should model behaviour and develop children's self-confidence and values of truth and right and wrong. |
| BEST VALUE | Settings should provide services efficiently and effectively, comparing costs with other similar settings and consulting with stakeholders to identify the best method of achieving outcomes. Settings should be subject to continuous review to ensure financial viability and a balance between cost and quality. |
| BUILDING ON LEARNING | **Children's ideas are the starting point for learning, focus on what children can do, not what they can't do.** Ideas from home should be used in the learning process. |
| CHILD PROTECTION | The welfare of the child is paramount. The environment should be safe and secure and the setting should identify a person to share concerns with. There should be clear methods of recording and referrals in line with local authority policy. Staff should have access to training and be able to identify signs and symptoms. Records should be confidential, and staff records kept up-to-date. Staff must be police-checked. A written policy should be given to staff and parents. |
| CHILDREN'S RIGHTS | Childhood is valid as a stage of life in its own right, each child is unique and their wishes and feelings should be respected as an individual. Children's interests should be fostered and followed to ensure they develop their full potential. Children should know their rights and have their opinions taken into account in decisions affecting them. They should be protected from anything that threatens their health, development and education. |

| COMMUNICATION | Information about the setting should be shared with parents/carers, staff, children and community. Parents and children should be listened to, their needs and rights considered. Staff should have good communication skills and be aware of verbal and non-verbal communication to be effective in developing relationships with children, parents/carers, other agencies and professional groups and to work in a team. Systems should be in place for ongoing daily communication, noting significant happenings. Communication skills are essential to the curriculum and can be learned through stories, songs and poems, drama, listening, music and literacy activities. Talking and listening are the main ways in which children learn. Positive communication should be used at all times and attention given to use of appropriate language and to users with English as a second language. Other means of communication, especially children with special needs, should be recognised. |
|---|---|
| COMMUNITY INVOLVEMENT | Provision should avoid isolation and reflect and belong to the local community. Information should be shared through groups, local networks. Settings can be involved in community planning/area planning and capacity building for childcare needs, and link with local community initiatives, liaise with other agencies, use resources in local community. There should be links with employers and other providers, and cross-sector/multi-agency partnerships including education and health. Schools have a significant role in the community. Group outings can be used to enhance links with the community. Consultation with users and local community can clarify expectations of services and encourage participation. Networking can share good practice. |
| COMPLAINTS | Settings should have a written complaints procedure known to parents, recorded and treated seriously. Settings should encourage and make use of comments and feedback from parents/carers. This should be linked to the evaluation system. |
| CONFIDENTIALITY | Records should be kept confidential and a confidentiality policy understood by all staff. Parents should have access to their child's records. Records may be shared with the statutory agency in the case of child protection. |
| CONSULTATION | Settings should consult regularly with parents/carers, children and the community to inform service development, the curriculum, ensure flexibility and access. **Policies should be agreed with all parties.** Local forums and newsletters can be used to promote ongoing discussion and information sharing. |
| CONTINUITY | Continuity should be ensured between settings and home and school. **The importance of continuity of relationships should be acknowledged, and respect for attachments given.** The care environment should be warm and consistent with continuity of staffing where possible. The key worker system can support this for group settings. |
| DESIRABLE LEARNING OUTCOMES (now Early Learning Goals) | **An explanation of Desirable Learning Outcomes should be available to parents/carers including the link with the Foundation Stage and National Curriculum and measurement of achievement by age five.** Desirable Learning Outcomes should be embedded in the curriculum, taught consistently, and staff should have access to training and guidance in this area. |
| DEVELOPMENTAL AGE and STAGE | Activities should be age (and stage) appropriate and promote social, physical, intellectual, language and emotional development. Staff should recognise that children develop at different rates and have different needs and interests and should aid the process of child development. Staff should have knowledge of child development and use observation and assessment to time intervention. |
| EMPLOYMENT | Settings should work with local employers to promote service, and meet needs. Family-friendly working practices should be promoted. |
| ENVIRONMENT | Environment includes layout, safety, maintenance and use of space. Work should be displayed and resources attractively presented. Staff should create accessible, labelled activity areas with space to use energy safely, child-sized fittings, room for floor-working, quiet activities and an outdoor area. Babies should have a separate space. Premises must be suitable and agreed with the regulator: heating, good lighting and ventilation, baby-changing facilities, storage, disabled access, readable signs, space for information display. The environment should reflect a concern for conservation of resources. |

| EQUAL OPPORTUNITIES | **Anti-discriminatory practice: challenge stereotypes and discriminatory remarks.** Multicultural practice: settings should reflect and celebrate cultural, linguistic and physical diversity and value different cultures through materials used, activities and attitudes. Parent and children's own names should be used. Settings should take into account the diverse needs of children and their families. All children have abilities and require the right conditions for potential to be met. Settings should ensure access and participation by all groups. Each setting should have a clear equal opportunities policy with full commitment to anti-discriminatory practice including recruitment and selection and monitoring of racism, sexism, homophobia, ablism, bilingualism, family norms, anti-bullying policy. |
|---|---|
| EQUIPMENT | Equipment should be regularly maintained to ensure safety. Multicultural equipment containing positive images of minority groups including children with disabilities should be used. Equipment should be relevant to stage of development and there should be a replacement policy. There should be easy access to equipment, which should be stored at low level and presented in an attractive way. Some equipment should be locked away for safety. Furniture should be of good quality and comfortable, and related to age and size of children. It should be easily accessible and of suitable height and shape. Hard and soft furnishings should be used. There should be a wide range of equipment that stimulates curiosity and meets the needs of children. |
| FAMILY SUPPORT | Parenting and pre-parenting education, advice and support including to single and younger parents can be provided by settings, family literacy can also be offered. |
| FLEXIBILITY | Settings should have flexible hours and programmes to ensure access. |
| FOOD | Menus should be displayed for parents' information and records of menus kept, menus should be developed through consultation. Menus should be varied, nutritious, meet cultural and religious requirements and respect traditions. Fresh fruit and vegetables should be used. Meals should be social occasions. Food hygiene certificate should be on display and staff should have training. Food can be used in celebrations. Babies must be attended whilst feeding and milk formula prepared by parents. Staff should understand the weaning process. **Children should be involved in menu planning and food can be used as part of the curriculum.** The setting should have a catering budget and undertake stock control. Staff should promote personal hygiene such as routine handwashing, and healthy eating. Children should eat with adults-using staff as role models. There should be a relaxed atmosphere during mealtimes and children should be allowed to eat and drink at their own pace. Staff should have knowledge of dietary needs. Staff should note what children eat to feed back to parents. |
| GROUP | **Children should have the opportunity to participate in small and large group activity to encourage partnership and cooperation.** |
| HEALTH | **The setting should have regard to the Health Improvement Programme and help address health inequalities.** Children's health is a shared responsibility between parents and providers. Settings should have a sickness policy which covers infectious diseases, emergency procedures, the administration and storage of medicine, personal hygiene of staff. There should always be a member of staff with a first aid certificate on the premises and a first aid box. The setting should have a separate space for a sick child awaiting collection by parents. Settings should promote health (parents and children) including exercise, nutrition, sleep, headlice, and should have a good link with the local health visitor. Providers should have access to specialist advice/child mental health services. Staff should have knowledge of skin and haircare. The impact of parents with ill health on children should also be considered. |

| HEALTH and SAFETY | **Health and safety procedures must be written in a policy and understood by staff and parents.** This should include accidents and incidents (records should be maintained), animals/pets, spillages, temperature of food provision and tap water. Fire regulations must be followed including regular fire drills, and fireguards used. There should be daily safety checks of the premises. Premises should be clean and hygienic with safe floor coverings, well lit with natural and artificial light, the rooms comfortable and ventilated, with sufficient space, equipment and lockable storage. There should be a separate rest space for children under 18 months, accessible toilets and handbasins, a changing area and individual face cloths for the children. Staff and visitors should have their own toilet. Children must be adequately supervised, and staff able to care for skin and hair and ensure protection from sunburn. Protective clothing should be available for staff and manuals to explain use of equipment. There should be a detailed plan in case of an emergency. Staff should operate a 'clean as you go' policy and premises should be cleaned when children are not there, toys and equipment should be washed, sandpit covered. Equipment should be kitemarked, stairgates in place, banisters safe, electric plugs protected, no trailing wires, safety glass used at low level, electrical/gas appliances checked regularly. Windows and doors should be safe and doors slow-closing. Care should be taken with noise levels, and the space should include a non-slip wet area as well as a carpeted area. Dangerous substances and rubbish should be inaccessible. Outdoor areas should be safe from the road, adequately supervised, greenhouses and ponds inaccessible. Settings should have access to a telephone and there should be no smoking anywhere on the premises. Settings should undertake risk assessments and have a named person for safety implementation. The kitchen area should ensure children's safety. |
|---|---|
| HIV/AIDS | There should be an HIV/Aids policy and good hygiene procedures. Information on support services should be available, and confidentiality maintained. Providers should have a family-centred approach and liaise with other agencies. |
| INFORMATION | Information on provision should be published, accessible and user-friendly (ESL and SEN). It should include admissions, settling in, written contract, names of staff and qualifications, admission criteria, hours of opening, fees, attendance and health rules, activities, routines, equal opportunities, assessment procedures, children with special needs, outings, policies, latest inspection report, advice for parents. Local information should be available through settings. Newsletters, networks and media can be used. Information should be up-to-date, training directories accessible, freeflow of information encouraged. Parents should have access to records. |
| INSURANCE | Insurance certificates should be on display, including employer liability, personal accident, contents, vehicle, building. |
| INTEGRATED | Care and education are inseparable and can link to family support. Care and education should link to other local plans and strategies for community services. |
| LEARNING and TEACHING | Staff should use a range of strategies to support learning and teaching which build on children's interests, stimulate curiosity, encourage experimentation and exploration using imagination. The curriculum should be broad, balanced, allow for freedom to learn from mistakes and use a variety of teaching methods based on the child's developmental needs. Staff should have high expectations of children and structure and support learning, combining child and adult-initiated activities. Adults create the environment for learning and support, valuing the process as much as the product. Techniques include use of artefacts, questions, discussion, making comparisons, using expressive arts, finding out from a range of sources, following instruction, imitation, investigation, ensuring links to the real world, problem-solving, role play, indoor and outdoor activities, active and quiet spaces, individual and group learning opportunities. Staff should give children opportunities to make choices and respond to efforts sensitively. Children learn from everything and do not separate into subjects. The curriculum should be planned to take this into account. **Observation and assessment should inform expectations for children.** Strategies should encourage the development of concentration, perseverance, attention skills and persistence including longer and |

| | |
|---|---|
| | shorter sessions for activities. Equipment should provide opportunities for sorting, pairing, grading, comparing and contrasting, matching, using size, shape, colour, texture, weight, temperature, sound, smell and form. Providers and/or keyworkers should know what each child has done each day. Children's discussion should be valued and community languages and linguistic backgrounds supported. Children's communication with each other supports learning. Staff should reinforce learning, and encourage reflection, extend knowledge and facilitate the application of skills in new situations, introducing theory for abstract thinkers and symbolism. Staff should have clear objectives for what is being taught and learned. Play should be spontaneous and freely chosen but structured at times. |
| **LEARNING EXPERIENCES** | **The following is a list of areas of learning which children should access:** BABIES 0-2: fixate on object/face, grasp fingers, watch hands, retain object, active response to hearing and seeing, increase movement to make something happen again, mouths object, holds/looks at object, reaches for object in view, searches for source of sound, reaches for/grasps object, hits objects, bangs objects on table/together, shakes/waves objects. LANGUAGE and LITERACY: written language, reading stories, phonological awareness, use of print, speaking and listening, reading, print awareness, recognising alphabet letters by shape and sound, name writing, using spoken language conventions, skills in other languages, organise/sequence and clarify thinking, sustain listening, respond with relevant comments and actions, interact with others, plan actions, extend vocabulary with the meaning and sound of new words, retell stories, confident speech, read familiar/common words and sentences, understand elements of stories: main character, sequence, understand information in non-fiction, and be able to explain where, who, why and how, hold pencil, make recognisable letters, correct formation, phonic knowledge to write words, guess complex ones, write own name, label, write sentences with punctuation, and write for purpose: list, story, instruction, make up stories, role play, meaning words /pictures, understand English reads left to right, that sounds are syllables, able to spell, developing library skills. CREATIVITY: REPRESENTATION/DEVELOPMENT: music, imagination, art, aesthetic appreciation, perceptual skills. KNOWLEDGE and UNDERSTANDING OF THE WORLD: senses, taste, technology, time, science, representation of ideas through different systems, computers, water, geography, history, design technology, IT, observation and investigation, solve problems, make decisions, predict, plan, question, explore, find out about environment, people, places, outings, visit, natural world projects, science: exploration, manipulation, observation, comparison, measuring, questioning, testing, patterns, seeking relationships, recognise features and objects, talk about objects, where we live in, living things similarities/patterns and changes, the purpose of features, record observations and explain them. MATHEMATICS: counting, recognising number, adding, subtracting, sharing, shape and space, sorting/classification, measures, shape, seriation, reason and logic, numeracy, skills of classification/discrimination/evaluation/sequencing, explore actively, introduction of symbolic systems, number, classification, measuring/ordering, space/volume, pattern. PERSONAL and SOCIAL DEVELOPMENT: different viewpoints, moral dilemmas, tolerance, spiritual, respect for natural environment, concentration, social skills, equal opportunities and anti-discriminatory practice, be able to co-operate, listen to each other, healthy eating, multi-cultural issues, personal hygiene (toilet/washing), express feelings, cope with difference. PHYSICAL: movement, muscular strength/coordination, control over body, spatial awareness, manipulative skills/hand-eye communication, gross/fine motor. ACTIVITIES: the home corner, small world play, construction: blocks, kits, natural materials: water, clay and dough, large and small construction, wet and dry sand, glue and make, hall, homes, helping at home, drawing, growing things, money, shells and stones, dressing up. OUT-OF-SCHOOL: homework: extra curricular support, experiences before and after school, family learning. |

| | |
|---|---|
| **LIFELONG LEARNING** | Early Years education should not be seen in isolation but as a foundation for the future. Settings should promote parents learning also: family literacy, parenting education as well as other training programmes. |
| **MANAGEMENT** | Settings should have adequate management structures including financial management, resource management and staff management. There should be job descriptions and person specifications for staff, contracts, disciplinary and grievance procedures, staff development and training programmes, induction, supervision and appraisal systems, team meetings, time for recording and evaluation, spoken and written communication between staff, parents and other professionals, staff cover and holiday arrangements. There should be a collective purpose and shared principles within the setting. Information should be available to support management structures, and long-term strategic plans based on identified trends should be developed and change managed where necessary. Staff, parents and children should be consulted in decisions that should be made on survey of need. Staff should be aware of their legal responsibilities and obligations. Clear management structures and roles and responsibilities will support smooth operations. **An annual report, business plan and audited accounts should be produced.** |
| **MARKETING** | Settings should provide information to the local community, disseminate good practice and help to raise the profile and benefits of childcare. There should be a publicity strategy. |
| **MONITORING and EVALUATION** | Providers should be committed to self-evaluation and review, setting goals and monitoring achievement. Inspection reports can be used to support this process as can observation and assessment reports, plans and records. Strengths and weaknesses should be noted and an action plan developed. Consultation with parents and children should be part of the evaluation that should happen on a regular basis and inform target-setting. Internal and external monitoring and evaluation systems should be used. |
| **OBSERVATION and ASSESSMENT** | Observation and assessment should inform the planning process/future provision, value previous learning and indicate progress. Adequate time should be allowed and observations shared with staff and parents. Methods used should be valid and reliable, fit for purpose and systematic. Records should be kept of observations and stored to ensure confidentiality. The role of the adult should also be observed. Children should be involved and ethical issues resolved. Baseline assessment is used to assess special needs and to inform pupil progress. Assessment should take place on entry to a setting. |
| **OUTINGS and TRANSPORT** | Well-maintained vehicles with suitable restraints should be provided with full insurance/MOT and staff should have a clean driving licence. Higher staff/children ratios should be used during outings. Parents must give permission for outings. Staff should know the community area and liaise with other provision/schools. **Road safety should be covered in the curriculum, routes planned, and children should have identification whilst on an outing.** Staff on the outing and at base should have a list of children, there should be a planned procedure in case of an accident. Children should have named escorts which have been police-checked and trained and have a contract of employment for collecting children. Children should be supervised in a vehicle and escort have access to a mobile phone. Outings should be fun and provide stimuli. Outings should be accessible to children with special needs. |
| **PARENT PARTNERSHIP** | Parents should be welcomed and involved as the prime educators of their children, design and delivery of service, settling in arrangements. Information should be given regularly to parents and carers, a two-way dialogue established and their role in children's learning developed. Effective partnerships between settings and parents should be developed. Settings can support parents' education through family literacy and other training programmes. Programmes for learning should build on home experiences. **Parents and carers should be regularly consulted.** Settings should respect languages other than English, faiths and cultural and religious customs. Parents' concerns should be treated seriously. Time should be taken to listen and talk to parents. Settings should ensure that they are flexible |

| | enough to meet parents' needs. There should be a clear understanding of the expectations of both parents and the setting in written format from the outset. Settings should involve other family members where appropriate. |
|---|---|
| **PARTNERSHIP** | Cross-sector/multi-agency working should include liaison with other settings and professionals, consultation with customers and residents, participation between sectors, providers, parents, communities and the locality. Joint planning and joint working should provide mutual support, a seamless service, training, regeneration, and networks through which to share best practice with a shared vision. |
| **PLANNING** | Settings should undertake short-, medium- and long-term planning based on observations and assessment and records of achievement, which involve parents and children. Plans should be regularly reviewed. Plans should take into account development stage of child, expectations, time, routines, goals and environment. Plans should be developed with children with special needs. Staff meetings should be used to review and discuss plans. Plans can be shared across agencies and sectors in the interests of transitions and partnership working. Training needs should be identified and planned for. Plans should be displayed or easily accessible and link to the organisation of the environment and learning outcomes. Planning should be part of the evaluative process. Plans should meet the needs of all children. |
| **PLAY** | **Settings should recognise the fundamental role of play in children's learning. Play should be active, structured, challenging, build on skills and understanding and supported by adults.** Play is important to make friends, feel good about self, self-confidence, experimentation, enjoyment, early science and maths, language and literacy, problem-solving, physical development. It can be quiet or noisy and messy. Outdoor and indoor environments should be used as well as cooperative and unsupervised play. Staff should observe play to understand the balance between play and learning. Play should reflect cultural diversity, be freely chosen with adults as partners. |
| **POLICIES IN PLACE** | All stakeholders should contribute to making/reviewing policy that should be written, accessible and clear. Settings should have the following policies in place: health and safety, recording and reporting, admissions, behaviour, equal opportunities, complaints, SEN, child protection, partnership, curriculum, parental involvement, emergency, fire, first aid, risk assessment, no smoking, recruitment and selection, observation and assessment, staffing, health, confidentiality, family-friendly policy. |
| **PROFESSIONAL DEVELOPMENT** | Staff should have at least a minimum level of qualifications and access to qualificatory training and professional development. **Staff should be encouraged to be reflective practitioners and time given to this process.** The supervision and appraisal process should support professional development. Staff should plan career development, have access to specialist advice, team building activities and networking opportunities with other settings. Staff should have access to up-to-date information and research and be encouraged to evaluate their own performance. Staff must have knowledge and understanding of child development. Induction programmes should start the process of continuous professional development and training plans should be developed individually and for the setting. Business competence training should be available to managers. Action research can enhance staff sense of professionalism. The impact of training on practice should be measured. Training for management committee members should be available. Multi-agency training should be encouraged. |
| **QUALITY ASSURANCE** | Quality assurance systems should aspire to a higher standard than the law requires, develop a commitment to a code of practice and enable high standards whilst maintaining the individual identity of a setting. Minimum standards should be developed for non-registerable provision. Systems emphasise self-appraisal and self-evaluation and standards can be shared across sectors. Targets for improvement should be set. **Systems should involve staff, management, parents and children and link to other policies and plans**. The aim of QA systems is to raise standards of achievement and attainment. QA systems should link to training and staff development programmes and promote good practice. |

| | |
|---|---|
| **RANGE OF PROVISION** | Choice for parents to reflect diversity and respond to a continuum of need. |
| **RECORDS** | The following records should be kept: children's achievements/progress linked to areas of learning, photographs, daily diary, attendance, accidents, medication, staff and volunteer details including qualifications and training activity, contacts in the community, other agencies, observation and assessments, child details, health details, details of authorised parent/carer, and contact in case of emergency, menus, fire drills, financial records, visitors' book, programme of activities and plans, deployment of staff, special events, a celebration of a child's life held between families, children and staff, records of achievement, financial records, entry, ongoing and exit profile. **Parents/carers should be able to contribute to records on children, and records be made accessible to parents.** Records should be factual in accessible language, dated and signed, and include the child's perspective. They should be manageable, useful and used, systematic, reliable, consistent, specific and up-to-date. |
| **REFLECTIVE CHILDREN** | Children should be given time to reflect, develop strategies, talk about experiences and practise new ideas in order to support developing independence. |
| **REGENERATION** | Childcare is part of economic regeneration in communities. Settings should participate in area planning, capacity building and anti-poverty strategies and can link to Welfare to Work and New Deal. |
| **REGISTERED** | Settings should comply with registration requirements and inspection regimes and other relevant legal frameworks. Certificates should be displayed. |
| **RELATIONSHIPS** | Relationships between children, and adult and child and adult and parent, and other agencies are essential to smooth and successful running of provision and central to development of children. Adults must be able to form and maintain relationships, understanding the needs and rights of others. Interactions must be positive and sensitive. Children learn awareness of others, communication skills, cooperation, conflict resolution and the effects of decision-making and choice. Adults' relationships with babies must be caring and close. Children should be able to initiate talk, share thoughts and feelings with adults and respect must be given to home language. Interactions should be warm, natural and responsive. Children should be listened to and spoken to with respect. Children should be welcomed by name and the handover done in a relaxed, friendly manner to ensure continuity of care between home and the setting. Children should be able to interact with children and adults in the immediate and the wider environment. Languages other than English should be respected. |
| **RESOURCES** | Resources should be maintained, be diverse, regularly changed, accessible and of good quality. Real objects should be used as well as toys and should match the age and stage of the children. Resources should ensure positive images and recognise cultural diversity. They should support language development, creative activity, role-play, quiet play, construction and outdoor play. Resources should be labelled and fit for purpose. IT resources should be available and resources which challenge stereotypes, are non-gender specific and in community languages. Centres can be used as a resource and there should be information about toy libraries. |
| **ROLE MODEL** | **It is the role of the adult to model behaviour, enhance and extend learning, stimulate, support and guide children and establish good relationships with children and adults (talking and listening).** Adults should enjoy children, be open-minded, reflective and responsive. Adults should be an advocate for children, give children time and space and respect their views. The adult role should be clearly defined and understood. Adults should be able to plan objectives for learning, space and resources, monitor and assess, keep records and evaluate. Adults should positively reinforce children's contributions, ensure each child is valued and promote each child's positive self-image. Adults should encourage risk-taking and independence but ensure adequate supervision. Adults should understand child development and interact sensitively and warmly with children. |
| **ROUTINE** | Planned daily routine should be ensured to develop a sense of security and stability, with peaks and rests tailored to children's needs. **Children's pace should be respected.** Routine should be balanced, clear and varied. |

| SAFE and SECURE | The environment should be safe, warm, stimulating and purposeful. Children and adults should give and receive affection. Settling should help children gain a sense of security. **Children's needs for love, food, warmth, shelter, happiness and the time of a caring adult should be met.** Premises must be secure, visitors should request entrance and sign in. Rest facilities should be available. |
|---|---|
| SELF-ESTEEM | Children's identity should be valued and feelings of self-worth encouraged to develop a positive self-image. Personal worth can be encouraged through conversation and practical activities. Confident children have a headstart in learning. Achievements should be celebrated and children given opportunities to extend themselves. Anti-discriminatory practice should promote positive images and children encouraged to express their feelings. |
| SPECIAL EDUCATIONAL NEEDS (SEN) | **Settings should follow the Code of Practice and be inclusive where possible, offering access for adults with disability, a flexible attendance policy, positive images, and a record of range of community-based services.** Staff should have access to training and specialist sources of support. Staff should be able to identify special needs early and ensure intervention and support. There should be an SEN policy and settings should have a higher staff ratio to support work with individual children. Importance should be given to partnerships with parents of children with special educational needs to share information and give support. Each child should have an individual record. |
| SOCIAL COHESION | Settings contribute to anti-poverty measures, social inclusion and support disadvantaged children and their families. |
| STAFFING | Staff should be 'fit persons' (Children Act 1989), and there should be a policy for student placement and volunteer helpers. The staff/child ratio should be observed. Staff should be easily identified. Keyworker systems can be effectively used. Staff must be police checked, in good health and references taken. They should have experience with young children, a relevant qualification, commitment to children and knowledge of child development, understanding of 'equal concern' and a positive attitude to race, culture, ability and behaviour management. Staff should be involved in developing policy and provision and their contribution valued. There should be qualified teacher involvement where needed for education of three- to four-year-olds. The supervisory structure should include supervision and appraisal, disciplinary and grievance procedures, emergency cover, staff induction, and non-contact time. There should be staffing continuity where possible and a clear recruitment and selection policy. Staff should have clear job descriptions, person specification and understand their role individually and in a team. Staff to be able to access training opportunities and uptake to be monitored. There should be a staff handbook and terms and conditions of employment understood, including payment of expenses. Staff records should be kept and staff encouraged to develop good working relationships with the team. Team meetings should be held. |
| SUSTAIN and INCREASE PROVISION | Settings should be sustainable and financially viable. Business skills should be developed. |
| TARGET IN NEED | Settings should ensure socially excluded groups have access to provision, including children in need and looked after, lone and low-income parents, children with special needs and disabilities, minority ethnic families, transient populations. |
| TIME and SPACE | **Children should be allowed time and space for practice, consolidation and extension of previous experience, to produce work of quality and depth, to explore and discover, for relaxation and quiet.** Children can be encouraged to make decisions about the time needed for a project. There should be time for rests and naps to reflect quietly and to speak and be listened to as well as to be noisy and boisterous. Staff to organise setting to ensure these opportunities are available. |

## Distribution of emphasis

By calculating the frequency of mention, it was possible to give an indication of the emphasis placed by each region and by the national materials on a particular Quality Area which could be aggregated to give an overall picture of the areas of consensus, difference and regional priorities. The patterns of emphasis are demonstrated in the tables below:

**Table 3.2    Areas of consensus (mentioned in over 20 per cent of materials)**

| Quality Area | Frequency of mention |
|---|---|
| Parent partnership | 55.5 |
| Equal opportunities | 48.3 |
| Environment | 47.2 |
| Professional development | 44.8 |
| Staffing | 43.4 |
| Learning experiences | 42.4 |
| SEN | 41.4 |
| Interagency partnership | 40.3 |
| Quality assurance | 35.5 |
| Monitoring and evaluation | 34.8 |
| Observation and assessment | 33.4 |
| Planning | 32.8 |
| Behaviour | 31.7 |
| Records | 31.4 |
| Learning and teaching | 30.3 |
| Child protection | 29.7 |
| Admissions and transitions | 29.7 |
| Information | 29.3 |
| Continuity | 27.9 |
| Food | 27.2 |
| Desirable learning outcomes | 26.9 |
| Health and safety | 26.6 |
| Community involvement | 26.2 |
| Relationships | 25.9 |
| Play | 25.9 |
| Equipment | 25.5 |
| Developmental age and stage | 24.8 |
| Activities | 24.5 |
| Access | 23.8 |
| Communication | 21.7 |
| Self-esteem | 21.4 |
| Integrated | 21.4 |
| Resources | 21.0 |
| Autonomy | 20.7 |
| Aims and objectives | 20.7 |

The following table shows the Common Quality Areas that have no mention at all in one or more regions. These are the areas which we have defined as having the least consensus overall.

**Table 3.3    Common Quality Areas not mentioned in one or more region**

| Activities | Group |
|---|---|
| Administration | HIV/Aids |
| Admissions and transitions | Insurance |
| Affordable | Lifelong learning |
| Aims and objectives | Marketing |
| Alone | Outings and transport |
| Atmosphere | Range of provision |
| Best value | Reflective children |
| Children's rights | Regeneration |
| Complaints | Registered provision |
| Confidentiality | Social inclusion |
| Continuity | Sustain and increase provision |
| Desirable Learning Outcomes | Target children and communities in need |
| Employment | Time and space for learning |
| Family support | Building on learning |
| Flexibility | Safe and secure |

A comparison between the overall frequencies and the frequencies relating to the national materials demonstrates the difference between the emphasis of the regional materials against those which have been developed by national quality assurance schemes.

The top ten areas of highest frequency of mention in the national materials and overall are shown in the table below.

**Table 3.4    Top ten Common Quality Areas of highest frequency of mention**

| National priority areas | % | Overall priority areas | % |
|---|---|---|---|
| Learning experiences | 72.7 | Parent partnership | 55.5 |
| Professional development | 59.0 | Equal opportunities | 48.3 |
| Interagency partnership | 50.0 | Environment | 47.2 |
| Equal opportunities | 50.0 | Professional development | 44.8 |
| Communication | 50.0 | Staffing | 43.4 |
| Parent partnership | 40.9 | Learning experience | 42.4 |
| Learning and teaching | 40.9 | Special educational needs | 41.4 |
| Environment | 36.3 | Interagency partnership | 40.3 |
| Community involvement | 36.3 | Quality assurance | 35.5 |
| Aims and objectives | 36.3 | Monitoring and evaluation | 34.8 |

It would seem that, whilst there are clearly common areas between the national and the regional materials, the regional materials emphasise the environment, work with children with special needs, staffing and quality assurance, whilst the national materials place significantly more emphasis on learning, professional development and communication skills. There are some areas that do not appear in the national materials at all as shown in the table below:

**Table 3.5      Common Quality Areas that do not appear in the national materials**

| No mention in national materials | % mention overall |
|---|---|
| HIV/Aids | 4.1 |
| Affordable | 5.2 |
| Flexibility | 5.2 |
| Employment | 6.6 |
| Family support | 7.2 |
| Best Value | 9.0 |
| Target children/communities in need | 10.3 |
| Regeneration | 12.4 |
| Lifelong learning | 13.4 |
| Atmosphere | 16.2 |
| Admissions and transitions | 29.7 |

Some of these areas relate to the emphasis placed on work with children outlined in the National Childcare Strategy and the guidance for Early Years Development and Childcare Partnership Plans. The data suggests that the regions are actually more 'joined up' in their thinking about services for children than the frameworks for practice developed nationally. There is more convergence in the thinking at national level about the areas of quality in some areas (demonstrated by the higher frequency of mention), whilst the regional data is more diverse and covers a broader spectrum.

There are different emphases placed on the Quality Areas by the different regions. The top ten areas and the lowest ten areas defined by frequency of mention are outlined below by region.

**Table 3.6    Top ten Common Quality Areas defined by frequency of mention**

| North West | North East | South West | South East | Yorks. and Humber | East | London | East Midlands | West Midlands |
|---|---|---|---|---|---|---|---|---|
| HIV/Aids | Family support | Building on learning | Building on learning | Administration | Administration | Marketing | HIV/Aids | HIV/Aids |
| Family support | Building on learning | Range of provision | Family support | Alone | Flexibility | Administration | Employment | Social inclusion |
| Marketing | Alone | Employment | Children's rights | Flexibility | Activities | Affordability | Range of provision | Confidentiality |
| Registered | Group | HIV/Aids | Administration | Sustain and increase provision | Regeneration | Flexibility | Children's rights | Administration |
| Insurance | Range of provision | Marketing | Range of provision | Registered | HIV/Aids | HIV/Aids | Affordable | Reflective children |
| Social inclusion | Safe and secure | Social inclusion | Employment | Activities | Insurance | Sustain and increase provision | Social inclusion | Alone |
| Building on learning | Marketing | Affordable | Safe and secure | Family support | Outings and transport | Employment | Best value | Flexibility |
| Alone | Registered | Administration | Reflective children | Affordable | Atmosphere | Reflective children | Family support | Complaints |
| Reflective children | Social inclusion | Health | Alone | Confidentiality | Best value | Social inclusion | Group | Atmosphere |
| Confidentiality | Reflective children | Confidentiality | Affordable | Group | Confidentiality | Range of provision | Confidentiality | Registered |

**Table 3.7   Lowest ten Common Quality Areas defined by frequency of mention**

| North west | % | North East | % | South West | % | South East | % | Yorkshire and Humber | % | East | % | London | % | East Midlands | % | West Midlands | % |
|---|---|---|---|---|---|---|---|---|---|---|---|---|---|---|---|---|---|
| Planning | 38.9 | Records | 38.5 | Professional development | 52.4 | Behaviour | 50 | Relationship | 43.7 | SEN | 46.1 | Play | 33.3 | Behaviour | 41.6 | Environment | 28.5 |
| Learning and teaching | 38.9 | Admissions and transitions | 38.5 | Desirable learning outcomes | 52.4 | Quality assurance | 50 | SEN | 43.7 | Parent partnership | 46.1 | Professional development | 33.3 | Admissions and transitions | 41.6 | Learning and teachings | 32.1 |
| Equal opportunities | 38.9 | Behaviour | 42.3 | Environment | 52.4 | Monitoring and evaluation | 50 | Parent partnership | 43.7 | Professional development | 46.1 | Information | 35 | Professional development | 41.6 | Information | 32.1 |
| SEN | 44.4 | Desirable learning outcomes | 42.3 | Partnership | 57.1 | Professional development | 50.2 | Planning | 46.9 | Environment | 46.1 | Planning | 35 | Monitoring and evaluation | 50 | Monitoring and evaluation | 32.1 |
| Partnership | 44.4 | Environment | 42.3 | Quality assurance | 57.1 | Equipment | 52.2 | Staffing | 46.9 | Partnership | 46.1 | Staffing | 36.6 | Equal opportunities | 54.1 | Equal opportunities | 32.1 |
| Professional development | 44.4 | Child protection | 46.1 | Monitoring and evaluation | 57.1 | Equal opportunities | 58.7 | Professional development | 53.1 | Children's rights | 53.8 | SEN | 36.6 | SEN | 58.3 | Staffing | 32.1 |
| Information | 50 | Observation and assessment | 46.2 | Staffing | 61.9 | Environment | 60.9 | Equal opportunities | 53.1 | Monitoring and evaluation | 53.8 | Partnership | 38.3 | Partnership | 58.3 | Parent partnerships | 35.7 |
| Observation and assessment | 50 | Parent partnership | 64.2 | SEN | 61.9 | Continuity | 65.2 | Environment | 53.1 | Learning experience | 53.8 | Environment | 40 | Staffing | 62.5 | Learning experiences | 39.3 |
| Environment | 50 | Equal opportunities | 50 | Equal opportunities | 71.4 | Staffing | 65.2 | Learning experience | 56.2 | Quality assurance | 61.5 | Learning experience | 40 | Environment | 62.5 | Professional development | 42.8 |
| Parent partnership | 55.6 | SEN | 53.8 | Parent partnership | 90.5 | Parent partnership | 65.2 | Partnership | 68.8 | Equal opportunities | 61.5 | Parent partnership | 43.3 | Parent partnership | 62.5 | Partnership | 46.4 |

Early Childhood Unit, National Children's Bureau

Consideration of the findings above shows that the South West consistently has the highest frequency of mentions for each Quality Area, whilst the West Midlands and London have the lowest frequencies. This indicates that, in terms of Quality Areas, there was most coherence and similarity in the South West documents, from whatever source, and most diversity in London and the West Midlands.

## Focus group feedback

The findings relating to the 69 Common Quality Areas and their distribution in terms of emphasis were fed back to each regional focus group. The key points raised in the ensuing discussion are summarised below.

Participants at focus groups were not necessarily representative of the authors of the materials and, as indicated in the previous chapter, were more interested in debating the broader issues of quality and their relationship to policy. Participants were given a list of the Common Quality Areas and asked to say individually whether they agreed with them or not, and to note omissions.

Of the 57 written responses received, there was little disagreement with the Common Quality Areas proposed, although two respondents were not sure that 'regeneration' linked with childcare and education and integrated practice. Some were concerned that children's services were in danger of being driven by employment concerns, removing children from the centre of attention. Others were also concerned that the Common Quality Areas should not be interpreted too mechanistically and that the importance of children's attachments, emotional needs and well-being needed to be explicit.

When participants were asked to cluster the Common Quality Areas into smaller groupings, there was some consensus on Quality Areas linked with learning such as 'active learning', 'building on learning' and children have the opportunity to play 'alone' or in a 'group'. Participants felt that these should all be included in 'learning and teaching' and/or 'learning experiences'. In other areas, however, participants clustered very differently from focus group to focus group, and demonstrated that there were a wide range of possibilities in the way in which the Quality Areas could be organised, depending on individual viewpoints and priorities.

One of the more debated issues emerging from the focus groups was whether the Quality Areas should be divided by areas of responsibility. Some felt that there were Quality Areas that applied at setting level and others at strategic/policy level — perhaps the responsibility of the Early Years Development and Childcare Partnership. Others felt that this was an exclusive view of integration, and that Quality Areas should apply as a shared vision across all stakeholders, but that their application would be different for a childminder, a setting working with children from birth to two-year-olds and at EYD&CP level for example. At one focus group, the Quality Area of 'autonomy' was hotly debated with regard to under- and over-twos. Some participants felt that the notion of 'autonomy' for under-twos was unhelpful, and that the focus should be on attachment. No consensus was reached on these matters.

Focus groups felt that some perspectives had probably not influenced the research. In particular, concerns were raised at the amount of material available for eight- to fourteen-year-olds and whether this age group was reflected in the audit. The extent to which playwork values were embedded in the research was questioned. Participants from EYD&CPs who were struggling to find a framework to encompass childcare from birth to age fourteen, commented that it was likely that most of the materials were developed to support work with a younger age-group. Other focus groups commented on the lack of materials for children under three. This is acknowledged to be a weakness in the research findings, but probably more because of the dearth of materials available to audit, rather than a fault in the methodology.

Individual regions were asked whether they felt that the pattern of frequencies for their region was valid. In the main, participants recognised their region from the frequencies mentioned, with the exception of the North East focus group. The East Midlands focus group was able to give an historical perspective on the high emphasis on 'regeneration' and 'employment' Quality Areas in their results. We had thought that it was, in line with other regions, a result of the National Childcare Strategy, but had been struck by the significance of the frequency of mention in the East Midlands. The group was able to give us a picture of the history of regeneration initiatives in the East Midlands as a result of the decline of the coal and steel industries and demonstrate the role that childcare had played in these initiatives over a long period of time.

Overall, focus groups felt that seven to eight Quality Areas that combined the 69 debated, would be helpful. These should not be too prescriptive in terms of implementation, but should give providers the opportunity to explain and express their own practices and provide ownership of quality at local level. Groups wanted to be able to build services and structures that were inclusive and locally owned, under the seven to eight overarching Quality Areas, shared as a vision across the country.

## The Eight Organising Principles

It was with this feedback in mind that we embarked on the process of defining eight Quality Areas. We decided to call them 'Organising Principles' because, as the focus groups had demonstrated, the 69 areas could be combined in a wide variety of ways. However, we do not wish to suggest that what follows is the only way of organising them. We needed to organise them in a way that we hoped would make them easier to retain, whilst at the same time embodying what we felt, particularly after feedback from the focus groups, were some of the aspirational aspects of the materials we had studied. The Organising Principles were as follows:

- Community partnership
- Documentation
- Equal opportunities
- Learning and teaching

- Developing citizenship
- Environment
- Health and well-being
- Staffing and professional development

The table overleaf shows how the 69 Common Quality Areas combined to make up these Organising Principles. It demonstrates where the Quality Areas and Organising Principles match with the 14 draft national standards (as they were June 2000) that were being produced as the project came to an end, and influenced the presentation of the project findings significantly in the latter stages.

## Table 3.8    Organising Principles

| No. | Draft national standards | Organising Principles for quality | 69 Quality Areas |
|---|---|---|---|
| 2<br>11<br># | Organisation<br>Partnership with parents<br>*Community partnership* | Community partnership | Continuity<br>Lifelong learning<br>Complaints<br>Consultation<br>Information<br>Parent partnership<br>Confidentiality<br>Family support<br>Employment<br>Partnership<br>Range of provision<br>Regeneration<br>Social cohesion<br>Admissions and transitions<br>Marketing<br>Community involvement |
| 10<br>12 | Behaviour<br>Care and learning | Developing citizenship | Behaviour<br>Children's rights<br>Self-esteem<br>Autonomy |
| 8<br>12<br># | Documentation<br>Care and learning<br>*Review* | Documentation | Records<br>Policies in place<br>Planning<br>Observation and assessment<br>Aims and objectives<br>Monitoring and evaluation<br>Quality assurance |
| 2<br>3<br>4<br>5<br># | Organisation<br>Physical environment<br>Equipment<br>Safety<br>*Sustainability* | Environment | Atmosphere<br>Routine<br>Administration<br>Registered<br>Flexibility<br>Safe and secure<br>Environment<br>Equipment<br>Resources<br>Health and safety<br>Outings and transport<br>Insurance<br>Sustain and increase provision<br>Affordable<br>Best value<br>Management |
| 9<br>14 | Equal opportunities<br>Special needs | Equal opportunities | Equal opportunities<br>Access<br>Target in need<br>SEN |
| 6<br>7<br>13 | Health<br>Food and drink<br>Child protection | Health and well-being | Health<br>HIV/Aids<br>Food<br>Child protection |
| 12 | Care and learning | Learning and teaching | Communication<br>Relationships<br>Integrated<br>Developmental age and stage<br>Active learning<br>Alone<br>Building on learning<br>Group<br>Learning and teaching<br>Reflective children<br>Time and space<br>Activities<br>Desirable learning outcomes<br>Learning experiences<br>Play |
| 1<br>2 | Suitable person<br>Organisation | Staffing and professional development | Role model<br>Professional development<br>Staffing |

\# Proposed additions

When we recalculated the frequency of mention in the eight areas, a huge consensus was evident. The table below demonstrates the percentages of frequency of mention overall and by region.

**Table 3.9    Regional frequency of mention overall by region (%)**

| | Developing citizenship | Community Partnership | Environment | Equal opportunities | Health and well-being | Learning and teaching | Staffing and professional development | Documentation |
|---|---|---|---|---|---|---|---|---|
| All | 67.2 | 74.8 | 63.1 | 64.1 | 47.2 | 79.3 | 68.6 | 78.3 |
| East | 69.2 | 76.9 | 46.2 | 69.2 | 53.8 | 76.9 | 53.8 | 84.6 |
| East Midlands | 75 | 83.3 | 70.8 | 79.2 | 54.2 | 83.3 | 87.5 | 87.5 |
| London | 62 | 70 | 53.3 | 46.7 | 41.6 | 65 | 58.3 | 68.3 |
| National | 72.7 | 72.7 | 59.1 | 59.1 | 27.3 | 77.3 | 68.2 | 68.2 |
| West Midland | 50 | 57.1 | 35.7 | 50 | 32.1 | 64.3 | 57.1 | 64.3 |
| Yorkshire & Humber | 65.6 | 87.5 | 65.6 | 71.9 | 43.8 | 81.3 | 71.9 | 81.3 |
| South West | 90.5 | 95.2 | 85.7 | 90.5 | 61.9 | 100 | 90.5 | 95.2 |
| North West | 55.6 | 72.2 | 72.2 | 55.6 | 33.3 | 88.9 | 55.6 | 72.2 |
| North East | 69.2 | 65.4 | 61.5 | 61.5 | 53.8 | 80.8 | 57.7 | 84.6 |
| South East | 84.8 | 76.1 | 80.4 | 76.1 | 65.2 | 91.3 | 82.6 | 87 |

Setting the project data against the draft national standards, there is significant commonality although the following elements are absent:

- Community partnership;
- Review;
- Sustainability.

Community partnership has been documented above, and needs no more explanation here. Review, however, refers to that part of the quality or planning cycle that ensures that evidence gained through observation and assessment, consultation and feedback, and whatever other monitoring processes used by a setting, is used to inform service development. This issue appears under 'Documentation' in our principles, but is not reflected in the draft standards. The area of 'sustainability' again does not appear as a single category, but as part of a number of Quality Areas that mention financial viability. Clearly, a setting that is not financially viable will not be able to achieve a number of minimum standards.

A calculation of the frequency of mention, isolating these three areas alone from their original Quality Areas, gives the following percentages:

|  | % |
| --- | --- |
| Community partnership | 74.0 |
| Review | 67.6 |
| Sustainability | 25.5 |

## National focus group feedback

The national group was asked to consider whether or not they agreed with the eight Organising Principles, how they could be used in a self-evaluation process and the support mechanisms that would be needed. The group debated the relationship between quality control and quality assurance and how the workforce could be motivated to move from a system of minimum standards that were quality-controlled to an aspirational vision for quality and a system of continuous improvement through a quality assurance.

The group broadly agreed the eight Organising Principles, but felt that much of the interpretation of the principles would depend on the value base of the interpreter and that this value base should be made explicit. Again, the issue of 'emotional warmth' was raised, and the group wanted this to be made more explicit within the Organising Principles, asserting that 'care' needed a fuller explanation than was currently evident. There was significant support for the need for there to be a way in which adults could acknowledge that love was an essential part of the experience of children. Nothing more, nothing less.

There was overwhelming support for the idea of a system of self-evaluation and self-appraisal derived from the Organising Principles, but participants wanted clarification on the relationship of the Integration in Practice Project with other kitemarking and accreditation schemes and with the emerging role of OFSTED in regulation. Participants were clear that systems such as the Local Authority Early Years Coordinators' Network provided the infrastructure for continuous benchmarking and that there was therefore a basis from which to begin to use the Organising Principles in a national system of self-evaluation. *Participants were united in the view that local ownership was key to the achievement of quality.* They were, however, equally clear that local ownership was possible within an agreed national framework driven by common standards or Organising Principles.

As the national feedback on the Integration into Practice findings demonstrate, there is not just a single static picture. Presentation of the findings has created a dynamic debate about quality and the nature of integration in current practice, exploring what can be aspired to. It has also demonstrated how, through evidence-based research, ideas about quality can be refined, challenged and progressed as the range of contexts in which this is played out also change.

# 4.    Examples of integrated quality frameworks

In addition to the audit of the content of the practice guidance materials, we have also considered the ways in which some Partnerships and their respective local authorities have combined their guidance materials into partnership-specific, integrated frameworks. Sometimes, these are referred to as kitemarks as in the case of Sheffield; in other instances, for example in Leeds, the unifying concept is a self-evaluation framework. Below, we describe the examples that provide an integrated framework of some kind in our sample and relate these to the discussion of approaches to quality in Chapter 1.

## Leeds

The Leeds *Let's Get It Right* (1996) self-evaluation framework is based upon a participative, inclusionary approach. (See Schratz's Matrix of Steering Options in Chapter 1). A participative strategy used to achieve quality development is displayed explicitly in the Leeds frameworks. The approach used is described as 'genuinely collaborative and corporate and based on agreed principles'. As Peter Moss argues in *Valuing Quality* (Moss & Pence, 1994) participation should be based on a broad range of stakeholders and a recognition of the values, beliefs and interests underpinned by definitions. In the Leeds exemplar, this is articulated by their genuinely collaborative approach that has involved comments, discussions, modifications and amendments by all sectors involved in the early years. The framework goes one stage further in that the language used in the documents has been agreed using a participative approach and has involved negotiation, agreement and careful consideration by a broad range of stakeholders.

The Leeds document is also an example of quality assurance in that the framework allows for a static approach whilst trying to improve performance. It offers a catalyst for discussion under dimensions of quality experiences and goes on to explore and identify gaps in provision and areas for development. Quality is seen as a 'process' rather than an 'objective statement'. The Leeds document describes quality as being 'like beauty is to some extent in the eye of the beholder. There is no one definition of quality'. The frameworks acknowledge that there are different views of the concept of quality: children, parents, carers, grandparents, providers all have a view. The framework suggests that 'children regard other children as by far the most important factor in determining the quality of their setting' (Moss and Pence, 1994).

They also include research from reviews of services for under eights that reports parents wanting more provision, which promotes the educational and social development of children, reliable standards or high quality in terms of curriculum, and well-trained staff. This process is considered of utmost importance in the Leeds model and encourages opportunities to explore, reflect upon and discuss values and objectives that define quality as a process. The document emphasises the need for regular review defined within a democratic approach in that all stakeholders contribute to the process. Self-evaluation is cited as the key to the improvement of the quality of care, education and play that children receive.

The quality assurance strategy that Leeds adopted is based upon agreed principles that underpin all early years education and care. The integrated approach to the framework brings together parent groups, voluntary sector, education and health representatives that feed into the process of agreeing underpinning principles. This process is again built on the system of participation and collaboration as described in the matrix presented by Michael Schratz in Chapter 1. The process is further supported by appointed quality assurance staff who act to support different types of providers. These have access to the developing Early Years Partnership Networks under the Family of Schools framework. This means that families will be supported by development workers and by the integrated early years team who facilitate local networking and dissemination of good practice. Another mechanism of consultation is accessed and developed through a quality and training subgroup that drafts guidance for all practitioners.

## Sheffield

The Sheffield Quality Kitemark (1999) has been devised through a bottom-up process with consultation and discussion from working groups. This is similar to the Leeds self-evaluation framework in that a participative approach has been adopted. In developing services for children and their families Sheffield describe quality as 'that which represents an essential strand and provides a major contribution to family support, partnership with parents and raising achievement'. The Kitemark was put together through a series of working groups and discussions whereby materials were constructed in the light of practitioners' own experiences.

The process demonstrates 'partnership in action' that draws on the strengths and skills evident in the various sectors involved. The materials were then piloted in various areas and intensive reworking of these was carried out. In the definition of quality used in *Quality Targets for Young Children* (European Commission, 1996) they describe defining quality as 'a process that is important in its own right, providing opportunities to share, discuss and understand values, ideas, knowledge and experience'. The approach involved in producing the Sheffield Kitemark mirrors this approach in that it engages people in a process of thinking that is ongoing, and the recognition of quality will be encouraged in this process of constant self-evaluation and striving for improvement. In bringing people together to look at their own values and practice, the process encourages the development of relationships with a range of different providers, rather than working in isolation or competition with each other.

Another essential element of the Kitemark approach is that it acknowledges that the situations in which people work are different but the essential questions about quality are similar for all. It also recognises that there is no simple, right way of doing things, 'It is the process of working towards quality which is important, inculcating the habit of constantly reviewing practice and being open to change, rather than the end product of the Kitemark'. There are elements that are high priorities in Sheffield that relate closely to the inclusionary model.

Emphasis on looking outside one's own particular environment and working with others, on involving parents and carers, and on equal opportunities make for a highly participative approach to quality. In line with the review of approaches in *Making Sense of Quality*

(Williams, 1995), Sheffield's framework is based upon the main components cited by Peter Williams as the foundation of quality assurance — that is: standards, indicators, evidence, systems, procedures and a commitment to self-assessment. Sheffield defines self-evaluation as 'examining what you are doing and why you are doing it'. This allows for participants to become aware of areas where improvements are needed and contributes to a continuing process of self-evaluation.

The three-year process culminating in the Kitemark has involved those who participate in becoming part of and carrying forward a continuous and conscious process to create a culture of striving for quality across all providers and throughout the city of Sheffield. The sharing of good practice and new ways of working will be shared through networks of communication. *The essence of the Kitemark is that quality 'is a journey, not a destination'.*

In line with the DfEE's requirement to use a partnership model, Sheffield has developed a community-led area planning process, the purpose of which is to bring members closer to the community. The planning process acts to promote the sharing of good practice in that it brings together providers on a local basis with an interest in early years in order for meaningful consultation to occur. It also acts as a route for accessing views of local parents. One of the key priorities outlined in the City Achievement Strategy was to integrate the efforts of all providers, including parents. By adopting a community-led planning process and working with local providers to produce Kitemarks, such as in Sheffield, it is possible to engage a range of strategies for improving the quality of services for young children.

## Bristol

*Author's Note: In response to feedback from practitioners, Bristol's Standard for Early Years was reworked and re-launched in May 2000. It contains more support materials to help people reflect and support their practice and is cross-referenced to the new guidance for the Foundation Stage. However, this report quotes from the Standard as it was last year.*

The *Bristol Standard for Early Years* (1997) is another example of an inclusionary approach, although not quite as explicit as the exemplars mentioned above. From the beginning of the work, colleagues from different early years backgrounds and settings worked together to produce the standard. A working group was set up to produce and develop the standard, made up of officers from education and Social Services and representatives from all types of early years settings, exercising an inclusionary element to their approach. This participative and collaborative process reflects a good example of partnership in action. As with the Leeds and Sheffield exemplars, the Bristol standard articulates quality 'as a journey, not a destination' and in this exemplar it is evident that they have approached quality as a process that is dynamic and shifting. It states that:

> ... a framework of this kind supports any setting in the process of continuous improvement and those involved commit to a process that demonstrates that they are a reflective, self-evaluating setting concerned with improving on existing practice.
>
> *(Bristol, 1997)*

The framework includes many of the components described by Peter Williams (1995) in a quality assurance approach including standards, indicators, evidence and commitment to self-assessment. The approach was to examine the relationship between quality and excellence and how this can be related to the jobs people actually do in early years settings. This was in order to achieve a more meaningful process for those involved in self-evaluation.

Although parents are not mentioned as part of the participative approach in this case, it is stated that the document should be widely publicised, particularly for parents to be able to make informed choices when choosing settings for their children.

The standard offers all settings a framework for self-evaluation, within which criteria are set in a continuum of improvement. It enables settings to identify where they are, where they want to go, and achievable targets to be reached along the way. The maxim for individual settings should be 'improving on previous best'. Within the definitions of dimensions of quality, the standards describe what should be challenged in the 'best settings', recognising available opportunities and making the greatest progress possible whilst continually improving on existing practice.

Local networks and subject-based groups feed into the partnership structure of Bristol. The Bristol standard is linked to working groups, curriculum frameworks and out-of-school provision. It emphasises the link to the DLOs in the curriculum framework (now the curriculum guidance for the foundation stage) and encompasses Children Act requirements. This is then fed into the Partnerships, formulating an ongoing consultation network. Other working groups, such as training and staff development, have key responsibilities to ensure assessment and validation of the standard. Objectives of the plan encourage all providers to work towards the standard and all training to be based around it. This encourages maximum participation in the framework and links the standard into a system of relationships that promotes local developments and formulates a community partnership.

## Isle of Wight

The Kitemark developed by the Isle of Wight, *Flying High* (2000), adopts a competence-driven strategy. Instead of the approach being based solely on an inclusionary model, whereby participation is based on as broad a range of stakeholders as possible, a competence strategy is defined by self-steering through professionals. The approach is expert-driven. Within this paradigm, the power distribution falls on a governing body or management structure of the provision, and the roles, processes and principles are driven by experts. Some inclusionary aspects have been identified in this model, in particular the document makes reference to and acknowledges that there are different views about the concept of quality. Close relationships between staff and parents and the involvement of parents in the running of the setting are cited as being essential in promoting quality education and care.

The framework includes components of a quality assurance strategy including standards, optimum levels of quality to be achieved, quality indicators that are matched against these standards and evidence to show how these standards are being achieved. Another aspect of an inclusionary approach evident in this exemplar is the formulation of a working party brought together to set out draft criteria for the kitemark and accredited scheme. This was developed through active consultation with childcare professionals, parents and children. In producing the document, cooperation from professionals and practitioners was a key element. This again demonstrates a participative, democratic approach.

The Kitemark includes a definition of quality to mean that 'children and adults feel confident, secure and safe in a welcoming, stimulating and caring environment where children's educational and care needs are met'. This is a clear example of what Moss and Pence state in *Valuing Quality* (1994) that 'quality is a constructed concept and subjective in its nature'. The standard also recommends a written statement of commitment and goes on to suggest that the commitment to quality 'must be shared and agreed with all staff and with all parents'.

The Isle of Wight's quality assurance strategy aims to support, encourage and promote high quality childcare and education provision. The intention of the partnership is to provide services that support staff in all settings to reach the highest standards. Quality assurance is one of these services. The Kitemark scheme is linked to the policy statement, 'commitment to quality', and also linked to regulation of settings and maintaining standards. To enable each individual setting to benefit from the self-assessment schedule, development workers and early years staff hold the responsibility of support visits and preliminary training for the scheme. This is further developed through arrangements of local professional cluster groups to build networking between maintained, private, voluntary and independent providers, including childminders.

## Cornwall

Cornwall's approach to quality, *For One Child and All Children* (Cornwall, 1999), incorporates a combination of competence-driven and participative elements to their approach. The participative nature of the work in developing the quality standards is evident in the documentation. A writing group was formed including representatives from the Early Years Service, the Early Education Team, Cornwall Childminding Association, PLEIAD, Pre-School Learning Alliance, National Day Nurseries' Association and the Youth Service. The writing group agreed the quality standards after discussing and defining quality from the point of view of different settings in the county. As with the previous exemplars such as Leeds and Sheffield, it is explicitly recognised within the standards that there are different approaches to the concept of quality.

However, the scheme does include elements of competence-driven strategies including the vision, values and aims of quality. The standards begin by saying that 'in best practice those involved with the setting will take part in drawing up the vision, value and aims'. This excludes stakeholders such as parents that would usually be involved in a participatory approach, such as in Leeds. It goes on to say:

> it may be created by one person for example a childminder or the owner of a private business who then spreads the vision to the others in the setting. Alternatively the vision may be drawn up by a number of people such as a committee or staff team.

> *(Cornwall, 1999)*

This gives a clear example of expert-driven values.

The standards contain eight areas of quality:

- vision;
- people;
- relationships;
- partnerships;
- planning;
- respect for one and all;
- physical environment;
- types of provision.

Providers are asked to self-evaluate under each of the eight areas outlined using a series of bullet points. From this, providers then complete an action grid which details future work to be done, and the time scales and cost factors involved. This information is submitted to a quality standards coordinator who decides whether a certain level of achievement of the quality standards has been reached. The Quality Standards panel consists of representatives from the Early Years Partnership and Strategy Groups.

The Cornwall Early Years Development and Childcare Partnership has developed a quality assurance strategy as a holistic approach to raising standards for children and families in the areas of care, play, learning, leisure and recreation. This shows an integrated approach to quality. The standards are explicitly written for all childcare, education and play settings. The standards apply to all settings and all childminders. The Partnership's aim is to achieve this through staff development, communication, community partnerships, creation of safe and stimulating environments and respect for every individual. All partnership training will link with the development and implementation of its Quality Standards for Early Education and Childcare. For example, Cornwall's training strategy group has produced a comprehensive training directory where all course providers are committed to following the Partnership's training quality standards that adhere to 'best value' principles. Quality assurance strategies of the Partnership are linked with the development and implementation of the standards.

The Partnership's strategy for disseminating good practice incorporates the development of agreed quality standards that are applicable across all sectors. Feedback to providers through Partnership representatives, extension of links between Early Years Service officers and development workers, joint training for providers from all sectors, production of curriculum materials for early years education by cross-sector working groups are all strategies employed by the Partnership which address the needs of an integrated system that provides for cross-sector working.

## Lancashire

Lancashire's *Guidelines for working with children under five* (1999) reflect a decentralised, competence-driven strategy. It includes some elements of participation in that a working group, representing a range of early years practitioners, produced the document. However, the process excluded other stakeholders such as parents. The document was devised to provide a framework for discussion and development between practitioners and to help develop relevant and appropriate guidelines that would encourage and support all aspects of quality learning experiences for every child under five. The guidelines quite clearly reflect a 'partnership approach', the document giving credit to people's contributions from the statutory, voluntary and private sectors. It aims towards Lancashire moving forward to a more coherent and multi-partner provision.

In particular, the following principles that the county suggest as underlying good quality nursery education, in whatever setting, seem of crucial importance:

- early childhood is valid in itself (it is part of life, not simply a preparation for work, or for the next stage of education);
- the whole child is important;
- learning is holistic;
- intrinsic motivation is valuable;
- autonomy and self discipline are emphasised;
- first hand experience (is the best way for children to learn);
- what children can do, not what they cannot do (is the starting point);
- there is potential in all children;
- adults and children to whom the child relates are of central importance (this is the responsibility of all who work with children under five).

They also cite a quote from the Early Years Curriculum Group (1989): 'high quality work with young children and their parents is based on important principles and founded on good practice'.

The framework contains areas of guidance including SEN, planning, parental partnership, play, the role of the adult and of the learning environment. Each area identifies a statement of excellence that is followed by a series of points that help practitioners identify areas of development, providing a framework for discussion. It aims to identify and promote elements of good practice and provision that are underpinned by the principles described above.

Through the development of the guidelines, the early years partnership seeks to develop and promote quality provision including minimum standards of service. Partnership with parents and a range of other providers across all sectors is a major strategy involved in the development of Lancashire's quality services.

## Rotherham

Rotherham's approach to quality is an expert-driven model. *Quality in Action* (1999) was created by a representative group of early years practitioners from the LEA, voluntary and independent sectors who worked together to produce this curriculum framework and self-evaluation document. The document is intended for use in a variety of ways including:

- to ensure children's learning opportunities are of the highest quality;
- to ensure parents have access to quality provision;
- to support and develop partnership across all sectors;
- to provide a minimum baseline quality standard;
- to support providers in the development of their practice;
- to ensure consistency of curriculum practice and care;
- to enable providers to evaluate effectively their practice and plan for future development;
- to ensure continuity and progression from each setting into the next phase of education.

The document aims to help settings review their practice against what the Partnership feels is a rigorous standard. As in this exemplar of a non-participative exclusionary approach, the practitioners are the experts who define the standard of quality to be achieved. All providers are expected to work within the standard and maintain at least the minimum standard that is outlined in the document. This is an example of a quality control measure suggested in Peter Williams's *Making Sense of Quality* (1995). The self-review linked closely with support, development and training is aimed at enabling each setting to build on its strengths and move forward confidently in the provision of quality service. The document sets out 11 sections for self-review. An action plan is devised from this evaluation outlining key areas for development within achievable and realistic time scales. The importance here must be the emphasis of building in time for staff to evaluate and review development.

*Quality in Action*, as well as outlining the Partnership's expectations of what constitutes a quality setting, is intended to serve as a curriculum support development document and links to the evaluation by providers of their own standards and to continuity of experience for children. It is also linked to the Partnership's training strategy. Joint quality standards are agreed between providers, funders and inspectors through the Early Years Provider Forum. Then a quality contract between LEA and provider should exist. The Training Strategy Group holds the responsibility of helping inform the training providers of the quality standards.

## Leicestershire

The *Early Years Quality Framework* (1999) devised by Leicestershire is an inclusionary approach. The working group represented participants of the Effective Early Learning Project and a small number of early years practitioners. It provides an integrated approach, offering guidance for all providers of care and education for young children. The framework is made up of sets of statements in relation to ten dimensions of quality. There is acknowledgement that not all elements relate to all settings, and that settings will have differing needs to address. This encapsulates a participative element to their process. The Leicestershire framework identified distinct texts that fall under the general title of 'quality' such as *Starting with Quality* (DES, 1990) and *Quality in Diversity in Early Learning* (ECEF, 1998).

Alongside the EEL project, the *Bristol Standard for Early Years* (1997) was used as a basis for the work. Guidance such as curriculum development handbooks and good practice sessional documentation were also used. As a starting point for the discussion of quality, as has already been discussed in Chapter 1, we know that these factors are all important elements. Similar to the Lancashire guidelines, there is consensus about underpinning principles that are good for children. In this exemplar, statements that are widely accepted as underpinning early childhood education, taken from *Quality in Diversity,* suggest that frameworks based on these principles will contribute to a more effective and coherent approach to quality.

On a second level we approach the Effective Early Learning Project Quality Framework (Pascal and Bertram, 1995). This framework is based on the views of practitioners, parents and young children within a range of settings and upon an informed understanding of research about how young children learn. There is an emphasis on the importance of the social context of learning and in particular on the role of staff in establishing this effectively. As discussed in Chapter 1, we know that it is generally recognised that the achievement of quality is largely determined by the actuality of the interactions between adults and children. We can see this is prevalent in a number of the exemplars identified in this discussion. The ten dimensions or aspects of quality relate closely to the Bristol standard and are intended to provide a broad overview of the quality of educational provision in any setting. These dimensions are not intended to be an exhaustive list! In looking at how they are actually achieved in practice, the framework suggests that 'in any practice these must be interrelated'. We can see here how the process undertaken by Leicestershire links to their aspirations for good practice. The dimensions are considered equally important, and all must be addressed to achieve quality. The aim is to support practitioners to improve on previous best through gradual change and development. It is used by following statements for self-checking under each of the ten dimensions. This allows for the practitioner to evaluate their own practice and identify future areas for development. A submission of a development plan will become part of the requirements of the Partnership's validation process.

At the time of writing the document, a consensus was emerging as to how the underpinning principles of effective action could lead to improvements of quality:

- judgments about quality need to be made;
- evaluation should emerge from an open, honest and collaborative dialogue using a shared vocabulary;
- this dialogue should be generated over an extended period of time;
- the dialogue should have a clear, systematic and agreed framework and format;
- the evidence for evaluation is gathered together and questioned together;
- the evaluation process should lead to action plans;
- the action should be followed through, supported and monitored;
- the setting should take ownership of the process and its outcomes;
- *all* participants in the process should be encouraged to make a contribution which is acknowledged and valued;
- an outside perspective is required and is most effective when the assessed and assessor trust each other;
- collaboration and participation are effective.

*(Pascal, Bertram and Ramsden, 1994)*

A key aim of the partnership is to improve the quality of all provision beyond minimum standards whilst expanding the range of availability. With the agreement of the quality standard a range of other practice initiatives are to be implemented. These include training and development opportunities, and the involvement of qualified teachers in nursery education settings, and the deployment of pre-school development workers. The district forum model offers providers of services opportunities to network and share good practice, resources and training. This network gives further opportunities for providers, individuals and organisations to be involved in quality development.

## Oxfordshire

The Oxfordshire *Quality framework for the Early Years* (1999) was developed using an exclusionary approach. A task group comprised of representatives from the voluntary, private and LEA sectors wrote the materials. The group was directed by the Partnership. This group holds responsibility for addressing quality issues in key areas of quality standards, support and monitoring. An important feature of the quality framework is that it is intended for use at various levels within the county, as follows:

- by individual practitioners as a tool for reflective self-evaluation;
- by headteachers, governors, managers and committees as a framework for planning appropriate provision and as a monitoring tool for supporting self-improvement in their setting;
- by local partnerships, as a set of agreed values about the needs of the early years community and as a shared agenda for professional development;
- by the Local Education Authority as a vision of high quality early years provision and practice and as a framework to support strategic, long-term planning for the early years. The framework also provides a common monitoring tool and an agenda for the annual review of early years provision by the LEA.

Practitioners and settings are encouraged to use the monitoring framework to undertake self-evaluation in order to establish a cycle of continuous improvement in early years. The framework sets out quality criteria that are the targets towards which all settings will be working. A deliberate decision was taken to set these targets at a challenging level in order for all settings to continue to improve on their previous best.

Following this process that Oxfordshire define as establishing a cycle of continuous improvement, there are specific strategies in place that make this possible. The Partnership's monitoring strategy plays a key role in how this process translates into practice. The county's early years adviser and members of the early years team have formulated a strategy to ensure the systematic application of the quality framework across all settings. In the maintained sector, quality is the monitoring responsibility of the schools' link advisers, all of whom have responsibility for a school partnership. In order to offer a similar level of support to the private and voluntary sectors, the Partnership has elected to appoint early years Partnership workers who would support and monitor the quality of provision and practice in these sectors. These workers come from all sectors of early years care and education and were appointed through rigorous criteria relating to experience, expertise and qualification.

Consultation with parents is another important part of the Partnership's work. When issues of quality are discussed, the needs and entitlements of children are paramount and Oxfordshire recognise that children must be involved in shaping quality standards. However, parents' participation was not included in the initial drafting of the framework. Other associations, in order to involve differing stakeholders in the process of sharpening the quality agenda within the county, have canvassed children's views.

As well as the roles of the quality and strategy group of the Partnership, additional subgroups such as training feed into this process. The recruitment and training of early years staff is high on the agenda in Oxfordshire. The county operates a comprehensive training programme that links with the quality framework. The self-evaluation process helps to identify current training needs and influences the overall strategies employed by the training task groups.

## Kirklees

Kirklees' *Quality for Young Children in Kirklees (2000)* illustrates a participative approach. Clearly evident in their partnership plan is that approaches to quality standards should be based upon the views of all stakeholders including children, parents, families, employers, practitioners and the local community working together to put the needs of the child at the centre of their concerns. They define quality as a dynamic process that encompasses a number of dimensions and all aspects of provision in all settings.

The main purpose of this quality document is to help practitioners self-evaluate their own practice and provision and to see how they might further improve it. There are 12 dimensions that have been defined under 'quality'. These are exemplified by a series of quality statements. Examples of important evidence are suggested and these are graded to help practitioners recognize and move beyond the minimum standards.

Much work has taken place in Kirklees through existing forums of providers, advisers and parents in developing a shared philosophy and approach to the development of quality provision for children. This relates back to definitions of quality published in *Quality Targets for Young Children* (European Commission, 1996) in that defining quality is a process that must be shared and that is important in its own right. Over previous years Kirklees have established cross-sector groups that have worked together on the development of a quality assurance programme based on self-evaluation that can be applied to all settings.

As has been previously discussed, a main component of any quality assurance scheme is key quality indicators that form part of the assurance documentation. Using a participative approach in drawing up these materials, Kirklees define six indicators that are fundamental in the process. These are classified as:

- the number of highly trained and experienced staff in a setting;
- the existence of an effective and well understood self-evaluation process;
- involvement of staff in ongoing training and professional development;
- effective management systems appropriate to the setting;
- sound policies on equal opportunities, health and safety, recruitment of staff and dealing with complaints which are implemented and kept under review;
- evidence from appropriate inspection reports.

Principles, including the UN Rights of the Child, are made explicit in all sections of the document. All these aspirations and regard for the fundamental rights of children must be linked to active mechanisms to achieve them in practice. As has been previously mentioned, it is these mechanisms that are sometimes not made explicit. Kirklees has an innovative track record in developing mechanisms for consultation. The partnership works with provider organisations to encourage the effective use of quality assurance materials. Out-of-school initiatives continue to promote quality assurance schemes. Development officers have been designated to support, help and provide further guidance to ensure improvements are made and sustained. Training strategies are linked in with the framework. The forums mentioned earlier represent parents and providers and take the form of a local network which contributes to the overall planning process. This will form a consultative structure and will further widen the stakeholders' role in contributing to the development of the standards. Kirklees is an exemplar of integrated practice, in their belief that the care and education of young children are inseparable. All services should strive to meet children's holistic needs in the areas of care, education, recreation and health.

## Oldham

The quality and standards subgroup of the Partnership has developed a local modular quality assurance framework within their *Early Years Development & Childcare Partnership plan 2000-2001* (2000) which will act as a 'stepping stone' between the minimum requirements of the Registration and Inspection Unit and the standards required by national quality assurance schemes. The modular structure has been developed to ensure everyone is fully represented in this process by a task group that represents parents, early years practitioners and childcare providers. This demonstrates a participative approach. Producing the quality assurance framework has been done in conjunction with work of the Registration and Inspection Unit as well as with other initiatives. The suggested framework links basic Registration Standards that currently exist, proposals for the development of the Registration and Inspection Units' standards and the local quality assurance scheme. This will in turn link with nationally recognised quality assurance schemes.

The Partnership has identified that support and intervention should have more immediate effect on the raising of quality. It intends to offer this through various ways including networking between early years practitioners in order to disseminate good practice, development officers to provide programmes of training, offering support to providers and parents. This will take place through active consultation processes to reach the widest possible audience.

A partnership forum has been set up to provide the opportunity for open, valuable discussion of all aspects of policy including quality and training. The Partnership has also developed a comprehensive training and recruitment strategy. This works through all stages of training and recruitment, starting at the grassroots level with community-focussed awareness rising through to accredited qualificatory training. In developing the modular quality assurance scheme and providing training support, the partnership aims to support the quality and standards group to ensure training and support are available to enable groups to achieve quality standards. Representatives from all key local bodies, including providers of training, employment and childcare, forms the training and recruitment group. This group reports to the Partnership and is serviced by officers from the early years team. Representatives on the group feed in and out to others as appropriate. This is an illustration of how the Partnership works strategically with local partners.

## Wolverhampton

The *Charter of Quality* (1999), produced by Wolverhampton Borough Council, takes a participative approach. The charter is organised into ten dimensions that are interrelated. Each dimension has a principal aim that is supported by statements of quality. These are then exemplified through a number of questions that give guidance on best practice. This is similar to the quality assurance strategies mentioned in exemplars such as Cornwall. The aim, statements of quality and questions relating to each dimension are set out on audit summary sheets. The setting uses these sheets to summarise and record a range of evidence related to current practice. There is also space for the setting to identify areas for development and subsequent priorities. Wolverhampton demonstrates an inclusionary approach here, as evidence that is collated is gained from various sources including observations, the settings' own policies, OFSTED reports and registration and social service reports. This evidence then forms the basis of discussions and evaluation with all adults in the setting, external support staff and advisers, for example, with teacher development workers and early years advisory teachers.

These dimensions relate to the 'ten dimensions of Quality' developed in the Effective Early Learning Research Project (Pascal, 1994). The ten dimensions are well known to those Wolverhampton settings that have already undertaken the EEL training programme.

## Cheshire

The *Early Years Framework* (1998) produced in this exemplar illustrates a participative approach. The framework has been developed by a group of representatives from a range of early years settings including social services, health, education and the private and voluntary sectors. Together they have set up a structure that acknowledges the interdependence of care and education and the benefits of professionals from different backgrounds sharing their skills and training. It also emphasises the need to help parents give their children the best possible start in life. The overall aim of the document is to set up a framework that clarifies and promotes appropriate early years provision across all sectors. It seeks to achieve this by:

- establishing shared understandings of children's learning and development;
- making a joint commitment to work together in the best interests of the children;
- encouraging access to appropriate shared training for staff, parents and carers which emphasises a holisitic view of children's learning;
- ensuring that the training is interactive so that theory and practice are developed together;
- informing parents of the framework criteria to enable them to have clear expectations for the provision of learning in early years establishments;
- fostering a genuine sharing of knowledge, expertise and information between all settings.

There are some participative elements to the process described above, such as achieving shared understanding, involvement of parents and the importance of shared dialogue which mirrors much of the DfEE guidance.

The document is intended for use for all those involved with care and education. It provides an opportunity to check the extent to which an individual's own setting meets the requirements laid down in the document. It is meant to respond to the needs of all children by guiding and supporting staff in their work with young children in their particular circumstances.

# 5. Examples of practice guidance within the 69 Common Quality Areas

In this chapter we illustrate the 69 Common Quality Areas, as set out in Chapter 3, by pinpointing specific examples of the actual materials which have comprised the formulation of the Quality Area. For example, within the common Quality Area of 'Food' we show an excerpt from the Sheffield materials which contained the principle that **'Children should be involved in menu planning and food can be used as part of the curriculum'** as highlighted in Table 3.1.

**Table 5.1     Examples of practice guidance**

| Organising Principles for quality | 69 Common Quality Areas | Example of practice guidance |
|---|---|---|
| Community partnership | Admissions and transitions<br>Community involvement<br>Complaints<br>Confidentiality<br>Consultation<br>Continuity<br>Employment<br>Family support<br>Information<br>Lifelong learning<br>Marketing<br>Parent partnership<br>Partnership<br>Range of provision<br>Regeneration<br>Social cohesion | Surrey<br><br><br><br><br><br><br><br><br><br><br>Derbyshire |
| Developing citizenship | Autonomy<br>Behaviour<br>Children's rights<br>Self-esteem | Leicestershire |
| Documentation | Aims and objectives<br>Atmosphere<br>Monitoring and evaluation<br>Observation and assessment<br>Planning<br>Policies in place<br>Quality assurance<br>Records | Wolverhampton<br><br><br><br><br><br><br>Bristol |
| Environment | Administration<br>Affordable<br>Best value<br>Environment<br>Equipment<br>Flexibility<br>Health and safety<br>Insurance<br>Management<br>Outings and transport<br>Registered<br>Resources<br>Routine<br>Safe and secure<br>Sustain and increase provision | Derbyshire<br><br><br><br><br><br><br>Leicestershire |
| Equal opportunities | Access<br>Equal opportunities<br>SEN<br>Target in need | Islington<br>Lewisham |
| Health and well-being | Child protection<br>Food<br>Health<br>HIV/Aids | Sheffield |
| Learning and teaching | Active learning<br>Activities<br>Alone<br>Building on learning<br>Communication<br>Desirable learning outcomes<br>Developmental age and stage<br>Group<br>Integrated<br>Learning and teaching<br>Learning experiences<br>Play<br>Reflective children<br>Relationships<br>Time and space | Cornwall<br>Bournemouth<br><br><br>Lambeth/next steps<br><br>Hertfordshire |
| Staffing and professional development | Professional development<br>Role model<br>Staffing | Cheshire<br>Lancashire |

> *'Admissions policy should be clear and issues such as routine of the child, routine of the group, expectations, payment and hours, holiday and sickness, bringing and collecting and settling in procedures clarified with parents at outset.'*
>
> **Organising Principle:**    **Community partnership**
> **Quality Area:**    **Admissions and transitions**
> **Partnership:**    **Surrey**
> **Document:**    ***Children First* (first produced 1993)**

The guidelines have been produced by Surrey County Council and have included contributions from early years practitioners, consultants and educational psychologists. They have been planned to be helpful to all those adults involved with young children within a diverse range of settings in Surrey. The purpose of the guidelines was to 'support the challenge of providing consistent high quality care and education for children wherever this is occurring'.

Under the Quality Area of admissions and transitions the guidelines set out issues for consideration by practitioners and relevant strategies that could be implemented.

Issues to consider for children beginning Nursery/Playgroup:
- change in routine;
- meeting the unknown-building, adults, children;
- level of self-help skills which have an effect on self-confidence and security.

Strategies to consider:
- having a named worker for individual children, and encouraging the parents to stay while the child settles;
- having a gradual build-up of the time spent in the nursery with parents present to support the child in becoming familiar with the routine;
- helping parents understand the need for children to improve self-help skills;
- having several visits before starting, and then a staggered entry.

Strategies to consider: (on entry to reception class)
- an admissions procedure which allows flexibility. This could include:
  - ensuring parents know and understand that they have the right to defer their child's entry if they feel the child is not ready for school;
  - admissions staggered on an individual or small group basis;
- as few interruptions to the children's time as possible. This is essential to foster the developing skills of concentration and perseverance;
- an evaluation is conducted with the parents of reception children each term to see if the induction process is meeting needs;
- the staff throughout the whole school are aware of, understand the need for, and support the development of, a sensitive and well-thought-out induction process for young children;
- ensuring that the reception staff have a sound knowledge of the child's previous experience and learning, either through visits or records.

> *'Parents and carers should be regularly consulted with.'*

| | |
|---|---|
| **Organising Principle:** | **Community partnership** |
| **Quality Area:** | **Parent partnership** |
| **Partnership:** | **Derbyshire** |
| **Document:** | ***Firm Footings* (1996)** |

In this approach the role of parents is valued as a significant influence in children's learning. The framework suggests that effective partnership between home and each setting should be developed as fully as possible. The following opportunities for parents are suggested:

| **Practice** | **Provision** |
|---|---|
| enter into a partnership with the school | facilitating a process of establishing relationships, for example home visits |
| understand that the education of their children is shared by home and school | collecting and sharing information by means of dialogue, admission profiles, sharing school policies |
| feel welcome in the school at all times | friendly relationships with staff helping with nursery activities and outings |
| share their expertise to enhance the learning opportunities provided within the school | for example, art activities, sport, music |
| have access to information concerning the school curriculum | by means of open days, meetings, discussion groups |
| having access to information regarding school policies | school policies for health and safety, records SEN, admissions, complaints, discipline |
| share in their child's progress and achievement | shared records, planned consultation sessions, displays of child's work |
| allow their child a smooth and flexible introduction into school | initial visit, information |
| continued and shared learning within the home | book library, resource packs |
| and from home to school | home/school diaries, sharing photographs |

*Author's Note: This document is currently under revision.*

*'The child should not be criticised only any unacceptable behaviour.'*

**Organising Principle:** **Developing citizenship**
**Quality Area:** **Behaviour**
**Partnership:** **Leicestershire**
**Document:** ***Early Years Quality Framework* (1999)**

This is again an example of an integrated framework of quality. It illustrates behaviour under the quality dimension 'relationships and interactions' and offers the following framework for self-evaluation:

- Adults are consistent and clear in their attitude and expectations of children's behaviour, providing a secure framework in which children can be encouraged to develop responsibility for themselves and others.
- Children are encouraged to value their own identity and take an interest in others.
- Children's needs are respected.
- Adults are aware that they are role models for the children in the way in which they interact with the children and with each other.
- Adults support children by respecting them as individuals, providing a positive ethos and helping them to build confidence in themselves.
- Children are supported in building trusting relationships with one another, so that they are able to share and take turns.

The following extracts underpin the quality dimension of relationships and interaction. This gives a theoretical and practical perspective of what is meant by the dimension and how this can be achieved in practice.

> This dimension of quality is about how well children and adults interact with each other. Those interactions, in turn, are dependent on the emotional well-being of all those involved. Establishing good relationships is fundamental in any setting. If relationships are positive and supportive almost everything else can develop.

> Early years workers carry a huge responsibility as key role models for young children, respecting and valuing people and behaving with dignity is essential. Young children are very perceptive at recognising honesty, trust and openness.

> If a child misbehaves in some way we need to ensure that our response makes clear to the child which part of the behaviour was unacceptable and why, and that it is the behaviour we are critical of and not the child.

> Children's self-esteem is profoundly influenced by the regard in which they are held by others and the way they are treated in day to day activities. Children are helped to understand how people and things change and influence their own and the lives of others by the way adults respond to the events in children's lives.

*'Underpinning values should be clearly stated and shared.'*

| | |
|---|---|
| **Organising Principle:** | **Documentation** |
| **Quality Area:** | **Aims and objectives** |
| **Partnership:** | **Wolverhampton** |
| **Document:** | ***Charter of Quality* (1999)** |

The Wolverhampton *Charter of Quality* has been produced through a programme of consultation with early years practitioners, members of the Partnerships and LEA inspectors. It is a quality assurance scheme produced by Wolverhampton County Council. The key purposes of the charter are to enable all settings to:

- provide quality education and care;
- raise standards of achievement and attainment in all areas of learning to ensure equality of opportunity for all children;
- support parents/carers in the education of their children;
- support attainment on entry to schooling;
- support the Authority's commitment to the concept of life long learning.

It mirrors the Effective Early Learning Project in that it aims to 'capture, accurately and rigorously, the essence of quality as it is reflected in practice and to explore how the individuals in each setting, including parents and children, perceive the experience the quality of education provided'. Under the Quality Area 'aims and objectives' this is described using a series of statements that underpin the quality dimension. Within each dimension questions are raised which aim to help providers identify areas for development and improvement:

### Aims and Objectives

An effective learning environment is provided when all the adults in the setting have a common philosophy and share their perceptions of children's learning. All partners involved with the setting should participate in drawing up and discussing the aims and objectives (for example vision, values and beliefs).

- Is there a clear set of statements of aims and objectives which is written down?
- Were the aims and objectives drawn up in collaboration and consultation with all staff and parents?
- Have the children been asked their views and have these been taken into account?
- Has other material been used to support their production i.e. research/literature?
- Has dissemination of the aims and objectives taken place to all staff i.e. have all staff received their own copy?
- Has consultation and dissemination of the aims and objectives taken place with staff, managers, other agencies, newly inducted staff, new parents?
- Is any other documentation to be attached to the aims and objectives documentation i.e. curriculum documents, QCA early learning goals?
- Are these aims and objectives referred to in other policies of the setting i.e. behaviour, parental and community links?
- Are these aims and objectives regularly reviewed?

*(Charter of Quality, 1999)*

> *'Parents/carers should be able to contribute to records on children, and records accessible to parents.'*
>
> **Organising Principle:** **Documentation**
> **Quality Area:** **Records**
> **Partnership:** **Bristol**
> **Document:** ***Bristol Standard for Early Years* (1997)**

The *Bristol Standard for Early Years* is an integrated framework of quality and is detailed in full in Chapter 4. This example illustrates records under the quality dimension, 'planning assessment and record keeping' and is illustrated as:

> This dimension of quality is concerned with how we ensure that there are planned as well as spontaneous activities within our settings. How we record what is important will also differ from setting to setting. In the nursery class it is more likely to be linked to the areas of learning and be a more formalised written commentary.

The self-evaluation framework incorporates the following:

**Record Keeping**

- All staff are encouraged to participate in record-keeping;
- Information is shared with parents/carers;
- Parents/carers are encouraged to make contributions to their child's record;
- Confidentiality of records is maintained;
- The following records are kept:
  - attendance register;
  - accident/medication/incident book;
  - information relating to the child;
  - observations;
  - assessments;
  - planning records;
  - staff records;
  - contracts;
  - dated samples of significant pieces of children's work;
  - profiles;
  - photographs;
  - other.

*Author's Note: The new version of the Bristol Standard was released in May 2000.*

*'Health and safety procedures must be written in a policy and understood by staff and parents'*

**Organising Principle:** **Environment**
**Quality Area:** **Health and safety**
**Partnership:** **Derbyshire**
**Document:** ***Firm Footings* (1996)**

Good practice in Derbyshire and the partnership between colleagues in schools and in the education department has formed the basis for *Firm Footings*. It is primarily a curriculum guidance document intended to support all those who work with three-, four- and five-year-old children.

It aims to support good quality childcare and education across a range of settings and focuses particularly on promoting continuity and progression for children. This example illustrates health and safety procedures, the need for a written policy and the understanding required by staff and parents:

- Basic rules for safety need to be understood and followed by all the adults involved, including nursery/reception staff, students, visitors, work experience school pupils, etc.

- Some rules will be pertinent to a particular establishment, while others will apply to all, in order to ensure safety at all times. Whenever possible, the school should liaise with families so that a child's clothing, footwear and jewellery do not restrict his/her participation in active play. Consideration should be given to the traditions and cultures of all these families.

*Author's Note: This document is currently under revision.*

*'Children's pace should be respected.'*

**Organising Principle:** **Environment**
**Quality Area:** **Routine**
**Partnership:** **Leicestershire**
**Example:** ***Early Years Quality Framework* (1999)**

This example was compiled by Leicestershire Early Years Team to support all those involved in the education of young children. It is based upon the developmental learning needs and characteristics of young children, the growing body of research on how children learn effectively and the good practice of early years educators throughout the county. It is intended to be used by any provider who works with three- to five-year-old children. Not all aspects of every area are appropriate for all settings but there is sufficient information within each area for any provider to identify with and use the plan for development.

The early years curriculum in this case is concerned with the child, the physical environment for learning, the adults involved and the strategies they employ as well as the content of the child's learning. Under the learning environment section of the document, the Quality Area routine is illustrated as:

> ... staff will need to be aware of agreed routines and expectations, young children need routine to develop a sense of security. It is essential to create an atmosphere which promotes self-awareness and encourages children to develop a positive self image by valuing the contribution that they make, praising and making positive comments to the child, encouraging cooperation and respect for others, respecting children and their families' cultural backgrounds.

The curriculum goes on to suggest planning for the internal organisation and use of space around the distinctive types of activity that will be commonly provided. For example:

- an area that provides rest and quiet;

- the need to socialise and talk;

- the need to make a noise;

- the need to concentrate individually and work in groups.

*'Anti-discriminatory practice: challenge stereotypes and discriminatory remarks'*

| | |
|---|---|
| **Organising Principle:** | **Equal opportunities** |
| **Quality Area:** | **Equal opportunities** |
| **Partnership:** | **Islington** |
| **Document:** | ***Guidelines: Inspecting For Quality* (1997)** |

The Islington guidelines, *Inspecting for Quality,* provides standards for the registration and inspection of full day care and education. It is a combination of Children Act guidance with LEA local educational standards and a list of statements representing the minimum standards to be applied by Islington Council. The document is aimed at for those who provide care to children under the age of five, whether it be an individual, partnership, a group, committee or voluntary organisation. It illustrates components of equal opportunities that include:

- Mandatory equal opportunities must be promoted for adults and children of both sexes with regard to employment, training, admission to day care, education and care service provided.
- Registered providers and staff should be aware of the provisions and prohibitions of:
    - Race Relations Act 1976
    - Sex Discrimination Act 1975
    - Disabled Persons Employment Act 1944 and 1958
    - Equal Pay Act 1970
    - Employment Protection Act 1975

- All daycare providers must ensure that, in offering services to parents, they do not discriminate against any particular parents on the basis of their race, religion, ability, gender or sexual orientation.
- Registered providers and staff must be committed to anti-discriminatory practice at all levels. They must provide an environment in which children can develop positive attitudes to differences of race, culture, language, religion, gender, sexual orientation and ability.
- All members of staff must treat the children and families, to whom a day care service is provided, with equal concern and, in doing so, must in the care that they give to each child, acknowledge and respect their specific needs with regard to their religious persuasion, racial origin, culture and linguistic background as well as gender and ability.
- All settings must show evidence of how they carry out the standards above. They must have an equal opportunities policy statement and guidance for staff members about how this should be implemented.
- Extra care must be taken by all members of staff when caring for a child whose first language is not English. This will mean working closely with the child's parents and ensuring that they and the child understand the routine and expectations of the setting.

> '*Settings should follow the Code of Practice and be inclusive where possible, offering access for adults with disability, a flexible attendance policy, positive images, and a record of range of community-based services.*'

| | |
|---|---|
| **Organising Principle:** | **Equal opportunities** |
| **Quality Area:** | **SEN** |
| **Partnership:** | **Lewisham** |
| **Document:** | ***Learning For Life* (1996)** |

Lewisham's *Learning for Life* is intended to be a practical guide to support all those working in education and care settings outside the home. It is intended for use as a tool for staff to evaluate and develop their practice and become reflective practitioners. Professionals from a range of services in Lewisham, including schools, early years centres and the voluntary sector have worked in partnership to produce this guide.

The document sets out practical advice and guidance in the context of a theoretical and developmental framework with key areas for the successful and achievable development and implementation of an early years curriculum.

Special Educational Needs, a key area in the document, sets out essential criteria for practitioners. It makes explicit mention of the code of practice as well as the involvement of parents in developing and implementing learning programmes. It is illustrated as:

As the code of practice says, it is essential to:
- Use information arising from the child's early years experience to provide starting points for the curricular development of the child.
- Identify and focus attention on the child's skills and highlight areas for early action to support the child within the class.
- Involve parents in developing and implementing learning programmes at home and in school.
- Take appropriate action, for example developing an individual education plan, and monitoring and evaluation strategies to maximise development and alert any relevant support or external professionals at the earliest possible stage.
- Ensure that ongoing observation and assessment provide regular feedback to teachers and parents about a child's achievements and experiences and that outcomes of such assessment form the basis for planning the next steps of a child's learning.
- Use the assessment process to allow children to show what they know, understand and can do, as well as to identify any learning difficulties.

It is essential that care is taken to ensure that the environment is sensitive to children with special needs. The curriculum should encourage open discussion and be informative about physical disabilities and other special needs. It is crucial that all children have access to the full, broad, balanced curriculum. Each establishment should develop its own special educational needs policy and refer to the Local Education Authority policy guidelines on the integration of children with Special Educational Needs. In addition to ongoing record-keeping and assessment, additional information should be gathered. This should include any advice from other professionals and close liaison with parents. Specific aims and goals should be set and reviewed.

> '*Children should be involved in menu planning and food can be used as part of the curriculum*'.
>
> **Organising Principle:**   **Health and well-being**
> **Quality Area:**   **Food**
> **Partnership:**   **Sheffield**
> **Document:**   ***Quality Kitemark* (1999)**

Sheffield's *Quality Kitemark* is an example of an integrated quality framework (see Chapter 4). It sets out a series of modules that provide questions for response. The extracts below are taken from Module 3 of the document, 'Meals, snacks and celebrations', and set out self-evaluation questions. Providers are encouraged to accumulate support materials after considering the self-evaluation framework. This then goes to a quality coordinator as a submission towards the Kitemark.

Under the Quality Area of food, this is illustrated in various sections and encourages the user to think about the best possible ways to approach meal times, how to involve children in this process fully and to articulate the aims that practitioners want to achieve from meal times.

> In every setting children receive food in some form, whether it is a brief snack or a full meal. Sharing food, and the conversation that goes with it, has been and still is a significant event in human culture all over the world, but modern western society risks the loss of many important aspects of eating together. Personal, emotional, social, intellectual and language development can all be promoted through well planned snack and meal times.
>
> We have a responsibility to see that all children participate fully in the whole process, and enjoy communal eating.
>
> Eating can be a very important issue for children with special educational needs and their parents. Independence in eating and drinking can be a significant goal for some parents.

The module is divided into five sections, each section offering questions for self-evaluation.

**Overall aims**
This section invites the practitioner to discuss and consider what it is they want to achieve from meal times and snack times.

- What do you want to gain from meal times and snack times, including children with special educational needs?
- Do you incorporate snacks into your overall planning?
- What is your policy on using food with regard to discipline?
- How do you work with carers to achieve your aims?

**A flexible approach to meals and snacks**

This section asks the practitioner to consider the best way to approach snack and meal times for their setting.

- How have you evaluated the system you use for meal times and snack times?
- Has this led to any staff development on the issue of the values and learning opportunities from meal times and snack times?
- Do you seek advice, look for new ideas and approaches?
- Can you give examples of when you have tried out different routines and strategies, who has been involved and how you have evaluated them?
- What is the role of the adults present (in what ways are the adults involved in meal and snack times and how do they interact with the children)?
- Do you constantly evaluate and review your policies and approaches?

**Children's involvement and development**

This section invites the practitioner to consider how they achieve the aims for the children in practice.

- How do your meal times encourage independence and the freedom for children to make decisions?
- How do children participate?
- How do your meal times promote self-discipline and caring skills?
- How do you ensure that your meal and snack times promote a relaxed environment that encourages social interaction and the freedom to enjoy eating?
- Have you as a staff team discussed what are socially acceptable eating habits?
- How do you ensure that meals and snacks promote good habits of personal hygiene?

**Meeting everyone's needs**

This section asks the practitioner to discuss and consider how they make sure that the needs of individuals are known and accommodated.

- How do you ensure individual needs and routines are catered for?
- How do you ensure a group approach to meal times whilst accommodating individual needs and preferences?
- How do you ensure that individual dietary needs are catered for?
- How does your practice reflect the requirements of the whole age range in your setting?
- How do you ensure that every child is being given the appropriate amount of support for their developmental stage to increase independence?
- How do you link snacks and meals into your community?

**The food provided**

This section asks the practitioner to think about the food they provide.

- How do you encourage cultural awareness?
- How do you ensure that children experience a wide variety of food, in a variety of forms?
- Does at least one staff member or planner have an understanding of what is a healthy diet?
- How do you ensure meals encourage healthy living and eating?
- How do you ensure that the presentation of food entices the children to eat it?
- How do you ensure hygiene standards are maintained?

Photograph by Adrian Rowland (National Children's Bureau, 1998)

'An explanation of desirable learning outcomes should be available to parents/carers including the link with the Foundation Stage and National Curriculum and measurement of achievement by age five.'

**Organising Principle:** **Teaching and learning**
**Quality Area:** **Desirable learning outcomes**
**Partnership:** **Cornwall**
**Document:** ***For One Child and All Children* (1999)**

Another example of an integrated framework is Cornwall's Quality Standard, *For One Child and All Children,* that is part of the Partnership's quality assurance strategy (see Chapter 4). In relation to the desirable learning outcomes, this example provides a curriculum framework as follows:

Settings should be providing a holistic approach to learning which is child-centred, delivering the Early Learning Goals. In order to develop children's curiosity, questioning, analytical and critical skills, we need to provide open-ended investigation and first-hand experiences within learning. The three to five-year-old stage is considered a distinct phase by Government. A new curriculum framework is being developed.

The curriculum framework refers to planned learning goals to be reached by the end of reception year. These goals incorporate the National Literacy Strategy and Numeracy Strategy. A curriculum framework helps staff to plan activities and experiences which promote children's development and learning.

- Children learn in a variety of ways. Adults need to ensure that a variety of teaching methods are offered to support that learning.

- Providers ensure the involvement of a qualified teacher in the setting who will act in an advisory role. Teaching takes into account the individual needs of the children, with a carefully planned programme of play-related experiences. Teaching will be lively, interactive, exciting and with a steady pace.

- Parents are seen as equal partners in children's learning and care and involved on a frequent basis.

- Delivery of the early years curriculum is child-centred.

- Early learning goals are delivered through a range of play opportunities.

- Play and learning is first-hand and enjoyable, providing a broad range of real and natural objects.

- Children's knowledge and understanding is expanded through topics and themes.

> *'Children should have the opportunity to participate in small and large group activity to encourage partnership and co-operation.'*
>
> **Organising Principle:**     **Teaching and learning**
> **Quality Area:**     **Group**
> **Partnership:**     **Bournemouth**
> **Document:**     *Quality Standards for Early Education and Care* (1999)

The Bournemouth *Quality Standards for Early Education and Care* illustrates opportunities for children to participate in group activities to encourage partnership and cooperation. This Quality Area comes under the organising principle of teaching and learning. The quality standards have been devised by the Bournemouth Partnership, that includes representatives from the quality assurance and monitoring group, teachers, early years workers and providers. The standards serve a variety of purposes. They are intended for use by parents and carers to assist them in making informed choices when choosing places for children, and also by providers to encourage self-assessment and target-setting within individual provisions and also by the partnership to monitor and evaluate the effectiveness of the standards in meeting their key purposes. The quality standards are based on the foundations and goals for early learning as described in *Quality in Diversity in Early Learning* (ECEF, 1998). Under the Quality Area of 'group' the standards include:

| Quality Standards for Early Learning | What it might look like in practice |
|---|---|
| Learning about their membership of groups and the possibility of being, at times, dependent and independent, acquiescent and assertive, of leading and following, in peer groups, family and community; | Children know the names of the people in their group.<br>Children join in and work in a variety of groups. |
| Learning about the groups (including ethnic/racial, cultural, linguistic, religious social) to which familiar adults and children belong; | Children are able to talk in front of a group and listen to others, e.g. in circle time. |
| Gradually learning about their membership of groups beyond their immediate surroundings; | Children show a developing understanding of the diversity of groups to which they belong. |
| Building on their first-hand experiences of belonging and connecting, coming to understand more about other people and other communities, past and present experiences and resources to encourage this. | Providers offer opportunities for cooperative group work and for individual work daily.<br><br>Providers offer time, relevant information, exploration of other kinds of groups such as cultures, religions, races, etc. Providers value all children as individuals so they have a sense of belonging to a group. |

> *'Settings should recognise the fundamental role of play in children's learning. Play should be active, structured, challenging, build on skills and understanding and supported by adults.'*
>
> **Organising Principle:** **Teaching and learning**
> **Quality Area :** **Play**
> **Partnership:** **Lambeth**
> **Document:** ***Starting Points* (1998)**

Lambeth's *Starting Points* has been developed through consultation between practitioners and outside agencies. It serves as a curriculum support document and sets out guidelines for all services working with children and young people. It recognises the role of development and training and acts as a starting point for that development. It also acts as a supporting framework and rationale for Lambeth Children's Services and aims to provide consistent levels of quality, entitlements for children and young people's learning, and continuity between services.

It recognises the fundamental role of play in children's learning:

> … play is an essential part of every child's life and vital to the processes of human development. It provides the mechanism for children to explore the world around them and the medium through which skills are developed and practised. It is essential for physical, emotional and spiritual growth, intellectual and educational development, and acquiring social skills and behavioural skills.

> Play underlies a great deal of children's learning. For its potential value to be realised a number of conditions need to be fulfilled:

> - sensitive, knowledgeable and informed adult involvement and intervention;
> - careful planning and organisation of play settings in order to provide for and extend learning;
> - enough time for children to develop their play;
> - careful observation of children's activities to facilitate assessment and planning for progression and continuity.

This example makes reference to the context in which children learn and states 'to create the context for learning there must be an acceptance that "how" children learn is equally as important as "what" children learn. This process of education is the principle which must underlie all curriculum planning.'

The Lambeth Early Years Development and Childcare Partnership is currently reviewing this document.

'*Settings should recognise the fundamental role of play in children's learning. Play should be active, structured, challenging, build on skills and understanding and supported by adults.*'

**Organising Principle:** **Teaching and learning**
**Quality Area:** **Play**
**Partnership:** **Lancashire**
**Document:** ***First Steps* (1990)**

The *First Steps* materials produced by Lancashire is an example of an expert-driven model. This piece of practice has been devised by professionals including teachers and educational psychologists. The documents are intended for use by parents (although this group was not involved in writing the document) as a guide for encouraging cognitive development through play. It is hoped the materials will foster a greater awareness of the stages of development of exploratory play. They have been principally designed to help children whose development is delayed.

Incorporating the already known fundamental principles that play and conversation are the main ways in which young children learn about themselves, other people and the world around them (*Start Right Report, Ball, 1994)* the materials are based on this context in which children learn spontaneously through exploration and experimentation gaining new skills and insight. The document emphasises the need for children to learn through the natural and enjoyable mediums of play and should therefore be given maximum opportunities to develop their play.

The document is intended for use as a checklist to assess the child's level of exploratory play. With this assessment taking place, one can use careful planning in order to develop the child's play experiences further. Activities are suggested for stages of development from birth to two-years-old including suggestions for appropriate equipment and materials that can be used.

> *'Relationships between children, and adult and child and adult and parent, and other agencies are essential to smooth and successful running of provision and central to development of children.'*

**Organising Principle:**    **Developing citizenship**
**Quality Area:**    **Relationships**
**Partnership:**    **Hertfordshire**
**Document:**    ***Hertfordshire Quality Standards* (1997)**

The *Hertfordshire Quality Standards* (a good practice guide for providers of care and education for young children) represents a practical approach to achieving high quality care and education in all settings. The document has been produced jointly by Education and Social Services and sets out principles that will help providers to develop and maintain high standards regardless of the setting. It is intended for use:

- as a framework for self-assessment by providers against which to measure their own standards and provision, and as a means whereby providers can work together raising their standards;
- as a means of providing guidance to providers through the registration and inspection processes, to support providers in addressing areas for development;
- to give reassurance and encouragement to providers by identifying and publicising good practice;
- as an accreditation scheme, whereby providers can be formally assessed and accredited as having achieved the standards in this document. This process will be developed through pilot schemes that will be monitored and reviewed.

The following points offer a framework for creating effective relationships between adults, children, parents and other agencies that are central to the development of children.

- 'The most effective adults are able to converse and interact with the child's experience without dominating' *Early Childhood Education* (Tina Bruce, 1989)
- 'Language and communication skills are of prime importance. Children should listen, interpret, question and demonstrate understanding and express their thinking in language' *Developing Nursery Education* (Julia Gilkes, 1987).
- The responsiveness of staff is a vital influence on children's progress in any pre-school situation, particularly with very young children who may be away from their parents for long hours and who need constant physical and emotional attention from staff, who are familiar with them and their non-verbal ways of expressing their needs. This will enable them to learn to cope with temporary separation that they will begin to accept as an ongoing process.
- Building relationships with other adults is important and needs to occur in a safe and caring environment where parents and staff work together for the well-being of the child.
- Communication that is sensitive to the needs and feelings of young children is essential. Adults should be responsive and enthusiastic with the children. Young children need time and support from adults who communicate easily and effectively by valuing children's contributions, giving the child time to listen and respond, providing positive comments and appropriate praise. These are the means of extending their thinking and understanding, behaviour and enjoyment.

*'Staff should be encouraged to be reflective practitioners and time given to this process.'*

**Organising Principle:**    **Staffing and professional development**
**Quality Area:**    **Professional development**
**Partnership:**    **Cheshire**
**Document:**    ***Cheshire Early Years Framework* (1998)**

Cheshire's publication, *Early Years Framework,* was produced to support and develop quality early years practice for nursery-aged children in all registered provider settings. It offers a clear and comprehensive account of all young children's needs and interests and all practitioners' range of responsibilities. It is intended to inform those responsible for the care and education of young children as well as to acknowledge the important role they play in children's development. The guidelines recommend the following framework for establishing and putting the principles into everyday practice:

- Share the principles for early years education with staff.
- Discuss each statement to make sure everyone understands its meaning.
- Decide which principles are the most important.
- Put these principles in an agreed order.
- Consider whether these principles are shown in the setting.
- Discuss findings with staff.
- Agree on setting principles.
- Write the principles down and display to all, including parents and carers.

One of the key principles described in the document relates to staffing and professional development. It states that 'quality care and education require well-trained educators/carers and ongoing training and support'. In order to achieve this, the guidelines offer a list of statements that contribute towards an effective quality early years environment.

    Early years staff need:
- continuing professional development that includes sharing of skills and research on early years practice;
- to monitor and evaluate their early years work continuously to improve their practice;
- appropriate early years qualifications, experience and training to understand the way in which young children learn;
- respect for the children's learning experiences at home, in the wider community and in other settings.

> 'It is the role of the adult to model behaviour, enhance and extend learning, stimulate, support and guide children and establish good relationships with children and adults'.
>
> **Organising Principle:** **Staffing and professional development**
> **Quality Area:** **Role model**
> **Partnership:** **Lancashire**
> **Document:** ***Guidelines for Working with Children Under Five* (1997)**

An example of an integrated framework is Lancashire's *Guidelines for Working with Children Under Five (1997)*. The document is for use by adults who work with children under five in a variety of settings. It was planned with the following aims in mind:

- to develop relevant and appropriate guidelines which will encourage and support all aspects of quality learning experiences for all children under five;
- to provide practitioners with a framework for discussion and development;
- to identify and promote elements of good practice and provision.

The framework, described under adult role, looks at suggested attributes that adults should possess when working in a setting. It goes on to recommend skills and attitudes of adults and the nature of their role when working with young children.

> It is vital that all those who work, or who are involved with young children, recognise the importance of their educational role and fulfil it. The extent to which adults working with under fives and their families possess different areas of knowledge will vary according to the role of the worker and the training they have received.

These are the suggested attributes which adults working in a setting should possess in order to provide a high quality educational experience:

**Knowledge and understanding**

- understanding of the way young children learn, their needs and characteristics;
- understanding the range and importance of play;
- understanding the way young children acquire language;
- understanding what is necessary to ensure the provision of quality experiences;
- understanding the factors easing transition and continuity of experience;
- knowledge of the earlier experiences of children, their home circumstances and any special needs;
- curriculum knowledge and understanding of appropriate activities and experiences for under fives and the ability to relate this to National Curriculum requirements;
- knowledge of recent research and the understanding of its implications in relation to the provision of quality experiences for young children.

**Skills**

- skill in planning and implementing the curriculum, in order to ensure breadth, balance and continuity with the National Curriculum;
- organisational skills and strategies for effective learning;
- observational skills and effective recording, monitoring and assessment of the curriculum;
- interactive and communication skills;
- management and leadership skills;
- skills in collaborative working with parents and other professionals;
- skill and ability to facilitate the provision of equal opportunities for all under fives.

**Attitudes**

- high expectations of children and self;
- genuine liking for, and sensitivity towards, children and a readiness to value them as people in their own right;
- respect for, and appreciation of, the contribution of other adults such as parents, colleagues and other professionals;
- a commitment to develop a partnership with parents with a shared sense of purpose, mutual respects and a willingness to negotiate.

# 6.    Next steps

Throughout this study, our findings have shown that everyone seems to want the same thing: the best possible services for children. Unlike goods produced on a manufacturing line, children are complex living beings, and the systems of quality assurance and quality control that support their learning inevitably reflect this. In the early years education and care sector, the 'goods' requiring quality assurance and quality control are the experiences of children and their parents. This is a system characterised by aspiration, which has multiple stakeholders and multiple layers of meaning.

In proposing a model of Early Excellence, in establishing the EYD&CPs and giving them responsibility for quality assurance, and in initiating the setting up of OFSTED as the national regulator for all early years and childcare provision, the DfEE have nailed their colours to the mast. The success of all of these initiatives relies, to some extent, on the integration of education and care. It could, therefore, be argued that just as education and care are often said to be inseparable, so are the project of integration and the project of achieving quality.

Integration in Practice has, therefore, sought to consider how practitioners in early years education and childcare in England understand the concept of quality. In so doing, the study has confronted a number of the central tensions in the current approaches to quality. Most notably, we have had to consider issues of empowerment, diversity and democracy. What does a partnership approach imply about the levels of stakeholder involvement? Is it possible to design sufficiently rigorous and robust mechanisms to enable consistent national scrutiny of one of the most diverse systems of provision in the world? Are there reliable measures sensitive enough for the multiple nuances of child-parent-practitioner interaction? We have sought not only to analyse the nature of quality as it is enacted at micro-level, but also to consider how activity at this level relates to the actions of government and its agents at the macro-level. Our conclusion has been that there are ways of bringing the most diverse and locally appropriate practice into a system of meaningful national comparison and that existing practice and thinking is available to support such a grand undertaking.

Integration in Practice has analysed much of what has been written by the community of practitioners in early years education and childcare about their aspirations for quality practice with children. By means of qualitative research methods, which have included 18 regional focus groups and one national focus group, the diversity of meaning in rich local practice has been distilled into 69 Common Quality Areas and eight Organising Principles.

What this has revealed is that 'integration' is a phenomenon that already exists and can readily be found in the hearts and minds of those who are driving the provision of local services. Integration in Practice has found that the traditional elements of education and care are continuously combined in guidance materials throughout the country. When describing how children learn, constant reference is made both to the complementary need for them to be 'safe and secure' and to the optimum conditions for teaching and learning which directly include parents. Whilst teaching and non-teaching staff may be sharply divided in terms of conditions of employment, and there may be disparate traditions within the sub-sectors of early years and childcare (maintained, independent/private and voluntary/community), these distinctions become less visible within the practice expectations set out by the Early Years Development and Childcare Partnerships and their respective local authorities.

Levels of experience and qualification do, of course, interact differently with such expectations. However, the fact that these sharp distinctions do not exist in the guidance materials suggests that integration in current practice is already a reality, but one that has yet to be articulated nationally. At the time of writing, OFSTED is due to become the national regulator by September 2001. As such, it will seek to develop a system of regulation that will engender uniform expectations of practice across setting types in England. Whilst this aim is undeniably welcome, we are left to wonder when OFSTED will begin to dismantle the differences in inspection systems for education and care. It will take time before the process of transferring staff from the local authorities can be effected, but there is an opportunity that we hope will not be missed to go much further than organisational integration. Our findings suggest that common national standards could be identified now for both education and care with setting specific additions to take account of parental choice and differences in the level of care offered.

Strikingly, our discussions have uncovered a frequently expressed view that there is a need for 'loving and caring' and 'emotional warmth' to have an appropriately acknowledged place in the care and educational experiences offered to children. Time and again this has been identified as a gap in the 69 Common Quality Areas. Nevertheless, the general response to these areas has been typified by coherence and consensus, rather than fragmentation and dispute.

Politicians and practitioners (if not parents) in England aspire to a seamless, holistic service for young children. In order to achieve this, in addition to a serious reform of the pay and conditions applied to early years and childcare practitioners, it requires the identification of a clear process for establishing an agreed *continuum of practice*. Such a continuum for early years and childcare would operate within an overarching framework for the achievement of quality driven by the principles of partnership and democracy. The DfEE has already espoused such a framework.

Having said this, the Common Quality Areas and Organising Principles identified by this report can be seen as a first set of signposts or benchmarks for such a continuum. If these are incorporated into an effective self-assessment mechanism applicable across all setting types, what begins to emerge is a way of bringing the myriad interactions between children, parents and practitioners into a formally acknowledged system of relationships within which all the key stakeholders understand their respective responsibilities in relation to those of others.

In the two figures below we have set out such a possible system of relationships and responsibilities. At the centre of each lies the eight Organising Principles, linking into national standards, national registration and inspection, diverse local practice and local (EYD&CP) systems of quality assurance – including mechanisms for self-assessment. In this way, the Organising Principles can provide an overarching framework to which everything else can relate: OFSTED inspection and registration protocols; setting-led self-assessment; Partnership led quality assurance, and so on. The net effect of this could be that a sustainable, locally expressed continuum of practice is replicated in every setting in England, directly linking local diversity and flexibility to vigorously applied national standards and systems of inspection.

The project revealed unequivocal support at local level for the idea of integrating rich local practice with rigorously standardised national systems of the kind expected to be established by OFSTED. However, both at national level and in the regions, participants were united in the view that local ownership was key to the achievement of quality. The ranges of meaning within the 69 Common Quality Areas express the current depth of local ownership. Participants clearly saw the possibility of having new, more focussed, ways of harnessing the strengths of this within a national framework. The system of relationships described in the diagrams below suggests such a way forward. The necessary controlling factor, however, is the establishment of a complementary and formally recognised self-assessment system within it.

**Figure 6.1     Possible ways of mapping complementary relationships between settings, Partnerships & OFSTED**

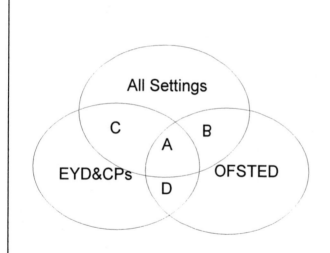

A)   Eight Organising Principles
B)   External inspection by OFSTED
C)   The local quality assurance
     process of the Partnership
D)   Information

**Eight Organising Principles**

- Community partnership
- Developing citizenship
- Documentation
- Environment
- Equal opportunities
- Health and well-being
- Learning and teaching
- Staffing and professional development

**Figure 6.2    Interactive responsibilities**

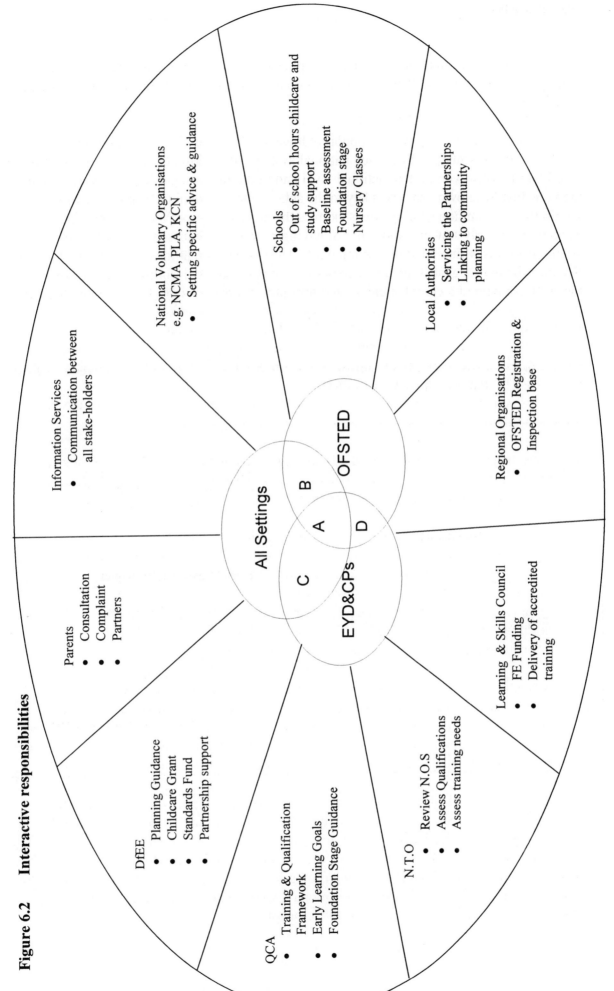

Early Childhood Unit, National Children's Bureau

# Building quality in the future

The evidence produced by this project has been collected within the Local Authority Early Years Co-ordinators Network. Established in 1987 and supported by central government grant, this network plays a significant role in the dissemination of good practice and is increasingly involved in the development of practice and policy. In a real sense, the Network is becoming a community of practice. We have therefore been concerned to maximise this potential, for example, by finding ways in which the evidence collected can be built on in the future. The technologies of the 21$^{st}$ century enable research and evaluation to be done with electronic assistance in the form of databases and spreadsheets. Sharing knowledge by means of computer-mediated systems is also routine and the internet makes it possible to network information, not only on a global basis, but also to do so in a manner that is structured yet responsive to queries. However, there is still a significant gulf between the implementation of policy on the ground and the systematic collection of the evidence which this implementation produces. Throughout the lifetime of this project, the Early Childhood Unit has been working to establish a robust and accessible interface between the networking process of the Early Years Coordinators and a web-assisted knowledge sharing forum.

This work is now completed. All of the findings of the Integration in Practice project are accessible on the internet within the evidence site of the Early Childhood Unit Network Support System at *www.earlychildhood.org.uk.*

The evidence contained on this website is structured using a table similar to that used in Chapter 5. The Organising Principles, Common Quality Areas and the related examples are linked in such a way as to enable comparison and review. These evidence pages will therefore provide assistance in the tasks of analysis, assessment, benchmarking and evaluation which are fundamental to quality assurance . The website will be organic, and as new evidence emerges it will be added, making it an ideal medium for comparison, continuous improvement and the systematic collection of information.

The interactive process will be advanced by other aspects of the Early Childhood Unit's Network Support System website, namely the open discussion board and local authority network database. These two dynamics, combined with the evidence site and the meetings of the Local Authority Early Years Coordinators Network, nationally and regionally, will enable the conversation on integration and quality assurance to continue into the new decade.

As a final next step, the DfEE has commissioned several pieces of work to bring self-assessment into sharper focus, one of which follows on from Integration in Practice. This new project – Quality in Practice – aims to build on the findings of this report and follow through the design of a system of self-assessment which can be used by all settings as a means of linking everyday practice and continuing professional development. In order to achieve this objective, though, there will have to be national ownership of the system, with both the Partnerships and OFSTED owning its development.

# References

**Local authority, social services and Early Years Development and Childcare Partnership materials:**

Bournemouth, Quality Assurance and Monitoring Group of the Bournemouth Partnership (1999) *Quality Standards for Early Education and Care*

Bristol, Bristol Standards Working Group (1997) *Bristol Standard for Early Years*

Cheshire, Early Years Framework Working Group (1998) *Cheshire Early Years Framework*

Cornwall, Early Years Service (1999) *For One Child and All Children*

Derbyshire, Advisory and Inspection Service (1996) *Firm Footings: The Derbyshire approach to the curriculum for three, four and young five-year-old children*

Hertfordshire, County Council Early Childhood Unit (August 1997) *Hertfordshire Quality Standards*

Isle of Wight, Isle of Wight Council, Early Years Unit and Early Years Development and Childcare Partnership (2000) *Flying High.*

Islington, London Borough of Islington Under Fives Service (1997 2$^{nd}$ draft), *Islington Guidelines: Inspecting for Quality*

Kirklees, Early Years Services (2000) *Quality for Young Children in Kirklees*

Lambeth, Directorate of Education, Lambeth Children's Services (July 1998 2$^{nd}$ draft) *Starting Points*

Lancashire, Early Years Development and Childcare Partnership (1999) *Lancashire Guidelines for working with children under five*

Lancashire, Educational Psychologists, Education Department (1990) *First Steps*

Leeds, City Council Under eights service (1996) *Let's Get It Right: Dimensions of quality education and care. A self evaluation framework for those working with young children in group settings.* The Council

Leicestershire, County Council Education Department (1999) *Leicestershire Early Years Quality Framework*

Lewisham, Early Years Curriculum Working Party (1996) *Learning for Life: A curriculum for the Early Years*

Oldham, Early Years Development and Childcare Partnership (2000) *Early Years Development and Childcare Plan 2000-2001*

Oxfordshire, Early Years Development and Childcare Partnership (October 1999) *Quality Framework for the Early Years*

Rotherham, Quality in Action Working Party (1999) *Quality in Action*

Sheffield, Quality Assurance and Training team (1999) *Quality Kitemark*

Surrey, County Council (first produced 1993 and revised over following years) *Children First: Surrey Early Years Guidelines*

Wolverhampton, Borough Council, Early Years Development and Childcare Partnership (draft) (1999) *Charter of Quality for Early Years*


**Other references:**

Ball, C (1994) *Start Right: The importance of early learning.* Royal Society for the Encouragement of Arts, Manufactures and Commerce

Barber, M (1996) *The Learning Game: Arguments for an education revolution.* Gollancz

Bertram, T, and Pascal, C (2000) *First Findings, Autumn 1999.* DfEE

Blenkin, G and Kelly, A eds (1997) *Principles into practice in early childhood education.* Paul Chapman Publishing

Brown, M (1990) *The High/Scope Approach to the National Curriculum: An introduction.* High/Scope UK

Bruce, T (1987) *Early Childhood Education.* Hodder and Stoughton

Bruner, J (1999) 'Each place has its own spirit and its own aspirations', *Rechild: Reggio Children Newsletter,* 3 (Insert)

Care Sector Consortium (1998) *National Occupational Standards: Early years care and education, levels ii and iii.* Local Government Management Board

Charities Evaluation Services (1997) *PQASSO. A practical quality evaluation assurance system for small voluntary organisations.* CES

Cordeaux, C and others (1999) *Child Care Training in the United Kingdom: Hera 2 Project - final report* (with Hall, B, Owen, S, and Miles, R). Suffolk County Council, Social Services Department

Council of the European Communities (1992) *Council Recommendation of 31 March 1992 on Childcare.* Brussels: The Council

Dahlberg, G, Moss, P, and Pence, A (1999) *Beyond Quality in Early Childhood Education and Care: Postmodern perspectives.* Falmer Press

Department for Education and Employment (1999) *Early Years Development and Childcare Partnership Planning Guidance 2000-2001.* DfEE

Department of Education and Science (1990) *Starting with Quality: The report of the committee of inquiry into the quality of educational experience offered to 3- and 4-year-olds.* Chairman: Mrs A Rumbold. HMSO

Department of the Environment, Transport and the Regions (1998) *Modern Local Government: In touch with the people.* Stationery Office

Department of Health (1991) *The Children Act 1989 Guidance and Regulations, Vol. 2 - family support, day care and educational provision for young children.* HMSO

Dodd, C (1998) 'A new class struggle', *Independent,* 4th March 1998, p16

Early Childhood Education Forum (1998) *Quality in Diversity in Early Learning: A framework for early childhood practitioners.* National Children's Bureau

Early Years Curriculum Group (1989) *Early Childhood Education: The early years curriculum and the national curriculum.* Trentham Books

European Commission Network on Childcare (1996) *Quality Targets in Services for Young Children: Proposals for a ten-year action programme.* Brussels: The Commission

Federation of the Highlands and Islands (1999) *Good Practice Guide for Out of School Care Projects*

Gilkes, J (1987) *Developing Nursery Education: From conflicts towards cooperation.* Open University Press

Glaser, B and Strauss, A (1967) *The Discovery of Grounded Theory.* USA: Aldine Publishing

Hammersley, M, and Atkinson, P (1995) *Ethnography: Principles in practice, 2nd edition.* Routledge

Holtermann, S (1992) (1995) *Investing in Young Children: Costing an education and day care service: A summary, [and] A Reassessment of the Cost of an Education and Day Care Service: A summary.* Early Childhood Unit, National Children's Bureau in association with the Association of County Councils, Association of Metropolitan Authorities and Voluntary/Statutory Young Children Group. National Children's Bureau

Kids' Clubs Network (1996) *Aiming High: Quality assurance scheme for out of school clubs,* (revised edition). The Network

Labour Party (1996) *Early Excellence:Aa head start for every child.* The Party

Malinowski, B (1922) *Argonauts of the Western Pacific.* Routledge and Kegan Paul

May, T (1993) *Social Research: Issues, methods and process.* Open University Press

Montessori Education (UK) Ltd (1995) *Montessori Curriculum*

Moss, P, and Pence, A e*ds* (1994*) Valuing Quality in Early Childhood Services: New approaches to defining quality.* Paul Chapman Publishing

National Childminding Association (1998) *Children Come First.* NCMA Approved Childminding Networks. NCMA

National Day Nurseries Association (1999) *Quality Assurance: Pilot Project.* NDNA

New, R (1998) 'Reggio Emilia's commitment to children and community: a reconceptualisation of quality', *Early Years,* 18,2,11-18

Pascal, C, Bertram, A, and Ramsden, F (1994) *The Quality Evaluation and Development Process: An Action Plan for Change. The Effective Early Learning Research Project.* EEL Project, Worcester College of Higher Education

Penn, H (1992) *Under Fives: The view from Strathclyde.* Scottish Academic Press, (Professional Issues in Education: 8)

Penn, H and Scott, G (1989) *Families and Under Fives: Report of a survey of 1,000 families with children under five in Strathclyde Region.* Strathclyde Regional Council, Department of Education/Glasgow College

Pfeffer, N, and Coote, A (1991) *Is Quality Good for You?* Institute for Public Policy Research

Pre-School Learning Alliance (1996) *Aiming for Quality: Accreditation Scheme.* The Alliance

Puffitt, R (1999) Excerpt from speech made at the *Best Value in Social Services* Conference. October 1999

Qualifications and Curriculum Authority (1998) *The Baseline Assessment Information Pack: Preparation for statutory baseline assessment.* QCA

Qualifications and Curriculum Authority (1999a) *Early Learning Goals.* QCA

Qualifications and Curriculum Authority (1999b) *The Review of the Desirable Outcomes for Children's Learning on Entering Compulsory Education.* QCA

Qualifications Curriculum and Assessment Authority for Wales (1996) *Desirable Outcomes for Children's Learning before Compulsory School Age.* QCA Wales

Rinaldi, C (1998) 'The thought that sustains educational action', *Rechild: Reggio Children Newsletter,* 2 (Insert)

Rinaldi, C (1999) 'Visible listening', *Rechild: Reggio Children Newsletter,* 3. p7

Salole, G, and Evans, J (1999) 'When ECD works: Mapping the contours of effective programming', *Early Childhood Matters. Bulletin of the Bernard Van Leer Foundation,* 93, 7-17

School Curriculum and Assessment Authority (SCAA) (1996) *Nursery Education: Desirable outcomes for children's learning on entering compulsory education.* SCAA

Schratz, M (1998) Papers from the *EVA: European pilot project on quality evaluation in school education* Conference, June 1998

Scott, J A (1990) *Matter of Record: Documentary sources in social research.* Polity Press

Statutes (1998) *Education Reform Act 1998.* HMSO

Statutes (1989) *Children Act 1989.* HMSO

Thomas, A (1999) *The Cynon Valley Project: Investing in the future.* Bernard van Leer Foundation (Early Childhood Development: Practice and Reflections. No 12)

United Nations (1991) *Convention on the Rights of the Child,* adopted by the General Assembly of the United Nations on 20 November 1989. HMSO

Wilkinson, J, and Stephen, C (1992) *Evaluating Ourselves: A self-evaluation package for pre-five services. An action pack for those evaluating the service they offer to young children.* University of Glasgow, Department of Education

Williams, P (1995) *Making Sense of Quality: A review of approaches to quality in early childhood services.* National Children's Bureau

# Index

## A

## B

## C

# G

government policy 3-4
groups 44, 91
guidance 6
*Guidelines:Inspecting for Quality* 85
*Guidelines for Working with Children Under Five* 68, 96-97

# H

health 44
health and safety 45, 83
health services 3
health and well-being 58-59, 77, 87-88
*Hera 2 Final Report* 12
HERA 2 project 28
Hertfordshire 77, 94
*Hertfordshire Quality Standards* 94
High/Scope approach 5, 16, 30
HIV/AIDS 45
home/school relationships 79

# I

information 45
initiatives, national 30
inspection 2, 13, 99
    *see also* registration
Institute for Public Policy Research 17
insurance 45
integrated quality frameworks 62-75
integration 45
Integration in Practice Project 1-3, 23, 27-29, 60-61
internet 102
Isle of Wight 65-66
Islington 77, 85
*Is Quality Good for You?* 17

# K

Kirklees 72-73
kitemarks 62-66
knowledge and understanding of the world 46

# L

LAGOS 25
Lambeth 77, 92
Lancashire 68, 77, 93, 96-97
language and literacy 46
league tables 6
learning 4-5, 46-47, 86, 99
        building on 42
learning experiences 46
*Learning Game, The* 5-6
*Learning for Life* 86
learning and teaching 45-46, 58-59, 77, 91-94
Leeds 62-63
Leicestershire 70-71, 77, 84
*Let's Get It Right* 62-63
Lewisham 77, 86
lifelong learning 47
literature 7
local practice *see* regional variations
'loving and caring' 99

# M

*Making Sense of Quality* 18, 64, 69
management 47
marketing 47
mathematics 46
matrix of steering options 24, 62-63
meals 87-88
meetings 29
methodology 27-39
monitoring and evaluation 47
Montessori Education 5, 30
Moss, Peter 18, 23-24, 62, 66